THE WILL OF THE PEOPLE

Its Formulation and Wise Use

Dr. Jean Pasquali

2018

MENTATION PUBLICATIONS

Arvada, Colorado

Published by Mentation Publications

http://www.mentationpublications.com

Printed by KDP Amazon

Copyright 2018 by Jean Pasquali

mentation@centurylink.net

Cover design by Daniel Ramon Bisque

Published in the Unites States of America

Library of Congress Cataloging-in Publication Data

ISBN-13: 978-0-9903511-5-3

Pasquali, Jean, 2018, The Will of the People: Its Formulation and Wise Use: Arvada, Colorado, Mentation Publications, 187 pp.

ON SOCIETY

Additional publications:

EL CIUDADANO TOMA SU LUGAR

EL GOBIERNO MEJORA Y LA SOCIEDAD FLORECE

GOVERNMENT AND THE SOCIETY IT SERVES

THE DIFFERENCE BETWEEN WAITING FOR POLITICAL DECISIONS AND MAKING THEM

LA VOLUNTAD GENERAL

SU FORMULACIÓN Y SU PODER

Figure 1. A photo of Ventura García, the man who taught me the expression: *"Two will bind a third one."* (See chapter *Inclusive Power*).

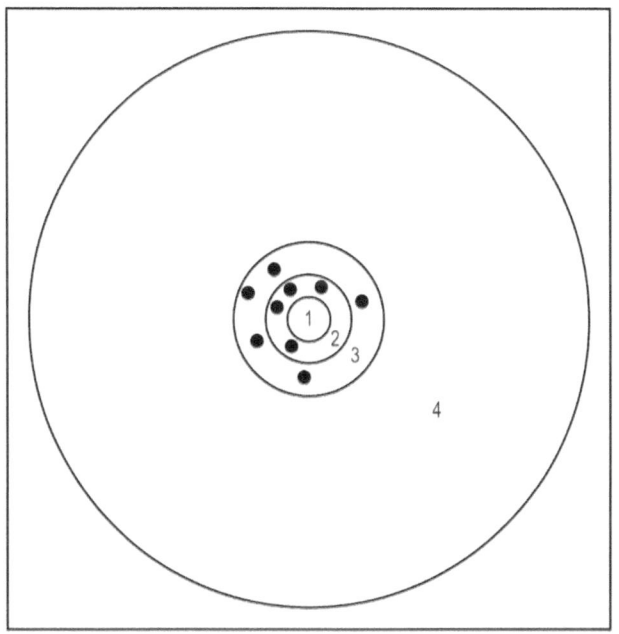

Figure 2. Size comparison of political powers in a country. Areas are proportional to the number of individuals associated to each power. Area 1 is the central power (nation or country); area 2 is the state power (state, province or region); area 3 is the local power (municipality, county or city); area 4 represents the sovereign power, which includes all citizens, who observe, discuss, lead, command, emend, and sustain the rest of the powers, continuously and collegially. (See chapter *Inclusive Power*).

CONTENTS

FIGURES

TABLES

DEDICATION

This book is dedicated to those that wish for an effective participation of all citizens in determining the responsibilities of government, the evaluation of its performance and the making of adjustments that are needed for the wellbeing of the population, as they arise.

The most common structural and operative difficulties that governments encounter are pointed out through the book.

The reader will be able to envision a new power that will guide and foster acceptable, beneficial and stable solutions that are specially designed for the needs of his society.

PROLOGUE

My interest in politics did not have an early start; it was stifled for a long time. Since my youth I have been listening to informal conversations where politicians were portrayed as cunny, opportunistic and dishonest people. The common recommendations included such expressions as *"make sure you do not go into politics"* or *"in politics, the bad people gorge on good people"*, or *"in order to be a successful politician you are required to know how to promise anything and everything and to steal quickly"*, or *"if you should get into that pigsty, you will not come out clean."* Perhaps such recommendations were prompted by my well-known propensity to criticize behaviors of people in positions of authority.

Later, in my line of work, I had the opportunity to observe up-close how critical governmental decisions were reached. They were frequently taken with scant information and without consultation. The selection of people for technical or scientific posts was frequently done on the basis of criteria that involved political rank or personal preferences.

The result, as it could have been expected, was that an important sector of the economy did not have the opportunity to develop on the basis of adequate and stable criteria. Other sectors received a similar treatment and destiny. As time went by the government distanced itself from Constitutional principles to such a degree that it caused a diaspora and a deterioration of the social order. This was accompanied by the decline of the economy, individual liberties and general wellbeing.

At this point, my citizen's duty convinced me to take politics as a study area. I was pleasantly surprised to find that many politicians, from antiquity to the present, have been keen researchers of society, profound minds that care about humanity, and developers of a clear perception of the relationship citizen-government-society. They are not anything like those that we commonly call politicians, when we should more properly refer to them as *vile politicians* or revive the archaic term *politicaster*.

How can it be that so much useful and easily attainable knowledge can coexist with so much ignorance or bad practice? I decided to investigate those general conditions under which current societies operate, in terms of what their members approve or disapprove about them. I followed the sequence: Observation, research, identification of evidence, possible solutions, proposals for actions, evaluation of probable achievements, foresight of difficulties, and reasons for urgency. Partial results obtained by following this sequence are found in chapter *Current Social Situation of Humanity*.

I went on to review the ways and conditions under which individuals develop, from conception or a bit prior to it, up to old age. I considered those situations that contribute to a healthy and happy life and those that act in the opposite direction. The results are shown in chapter *Individual Development.*

I attempted to associate those social conditions of the individual, be them positive or negative, that depend on a considerable degree on responsibilities, direction and structure of government. The relationships that I believe could and should exist between governmental functions and government power structures are treated in chapter *Favorable Structures.*

In the chapter *Political Toxicology,* the most common symptoms or indicators of undesirable conditions for the individual, which are derived from his dependence on government or society, are described. The subject matter of this chapter is the closest to traditional politics with which we may have gotten accustomed. The unfortunately common and negative relationship between the citizen and his government is considered. At the same time, ways to improve such relationships are presented.

In order to insert changes into the present state of affairs it should be understood why the high-quality knowledge that is readily available is not used. How is it possible for it to coexist with a way to do politics that is being so questioned and, generally, so inadequate for the needs of the citizenry? On Earth there are, at the present time, around two hundred governments of nation-states. Although their responsibilities are similar, each one is unique; while a few are very different from the rest. It is possible to recognize among them, those that are better than most, and those that are especially deficient (Chandy, 2017). To a first approximation, those that work better are those that belong to countries with high productivity and a population with a high educational level.

Government is a system. It has a set of principles and rules, rationally integrated, that contribute to the fulfillment of its responsibilities. The evaluation of a government's success requires the study of its principles, rules and the purpose of its existence.

The determination of what is expected from a county's government, with the specification of the breath and the limits of its responsibilities, is a process needed for the creation of its structure. It should be adapted to its functions. The purpose of government for each country has been determined by its culture and its history. Such an origin implies that it has been mostly developed by people of past generations. Due to internal changes undergone by societies, the production of new knowledge in all areas and the modification of international settings, it is probable that the purpose of governments requires a meaningful adjustment. If that should be the case, populations would now be suffering the negative effects of obsolescence and giving support to structures that are not adequate for present circumstances.

This situation brings to bear the need and the advantages to formally introduce the periodic review and, perhaps, adjustment or modification of the purpose of government. Better yet would be to introduce adjustments to the purpose of government, as new relevant knowledge is produced, or new international settings come to be, or preferences of the population change considerably. It is easy to see, how countries in which these changes or adjustments are added as part of their Constitution, will have advantages over others who do not.

It could also be that the current government system, with its principles and laws, has reached a point in which it is impossible to introduce significant changes to its purpose. In such case a new system has to be established; hopefully by peaceful means. Excellent examples indicate or prove that such changes are viable.

I was under the impression that principles of a country's government system would be very similar in all countries and include maintenance of social order and fostering wellbeing in the population. That is not so. There are countries that have a Constitution that has been devised on the basis of ideas that belong to an historical figure or derived from dogmas of a religion or from political ideologies of different origins. They are systems with rules, principles, methods or practices that make the free expression of current citizens' needs or preferences difficult or unwelcomed. In some cases, those restrictions can even produce strained relations between nations.

In chapter *Inclusive Power*, a process that will serve to establish and defend—in a continuous fashion—the political rights of each member of society is described. This process, independently of the country's history, traditions, cultures, religions, myths, legends, rituals, taboos and ideologies will foster the wellbeing and happiness of the population and provide stability.

The proposed procedure or system has its origin on the consideration of answers to questions such as: Who decides?; Who governs?; Who has the power to dispute decisions?; Who may nullify decisions?; When can decisions be disputed, nullified or imposed?; Who determines the responsibilities of government?; Who can introduce adjustments to the purpose of government?; What changes are achievable in one generation?; Are most of the capitals at hand— human, social, economic and environmental—being utilized?; Are there acceptable and effective methods to reach political decisions by the use of the collective intelligence of citizens?; Which are the main obstacles to the improvement of the development of the individual?.

I have no intent here to determine the purpose of any government, since each society has different and unique needs. They are determined by the situation and the preferences of its citizens. Precisely, for this reason, each society has to determine, on the basis of its present status, what it wishes to achieve. Without such determination society is adrift.

The questions posed above are applicable to countries, states, cities, municipalities, and other associations such as nations and tribes, union of countries, and the much-discussed global government.

My *intent* is to ensure that the resulting purpose of government will preserve the individual power to control his personal development and to participate in collective initiatives related to government matters, under equivalent conditions to those of any other citizen.

This book could be useful to people that wish to critically and constructively analyze their government.

INTRODUCTION

"It is change, the continuous change, the inevitable change, that is the dominant factor in society today. No sensible decision can be made any longer without taking into account not only the world as it is but the world as it will be."

Isaac Asimov (1920-1992)

The daring historian David Priestland, modern history professor at the University of Oxford, has undertaken the challenge to study the ways in which different parts of society have exchanged positions acting as the forces that fostered historical changes, during the last ten thousand years (Priestland, 2013). These components or fractions of society have been called *castes* and there are four of them: 1. Aristocrats and soldiers; 2. Sages and priests; 3. Merchants; and 4. Peasants, artisans and proletarians.

The fact that three of these castes have taken turns in "power" may be useful to identify the causes that made them reach or lose power and to determine if there is such a thing as an intrinsic instability in human societies as we know them today. It may also be useful to envision if it should be feasible to foster or prevent those social disruptions that commonly take place when power changes hands.

A general consideration of living beings finds that the drive to better their situation is common to all of them. It is a tendency that takes many different forms depending on the being and the moment.

For example, unicellular organisms seem to be constantly hungry. It is entertaining to look through a microscope a water sample taken from a vase that contains an aquatic plant. Single-cell beings of different species keep themselves busy escaping from those that want to eat them and pursuing those that let themselves be caught. At this social level, success means being alive, and failure means ceasing to be.

An interesting paleontological development is the appearance of multicellular beings. In them many cells combine, in an orderly fashion, to build an organism where sets of cells have characteristic functions. These allow the organism to make use of resources that are not available to unicellular organisms, because of size, composition, position, mobility, structure et cetera. In these beings, relationships of dependence and collaboration among group of cells make possible the development of complex actions and behaviors by the whole.

For example, the seeds of trees in a tropical jungle, if they should be able to reach germination, they will have one group of cells dedicated to go downward and build a system of roots, and another to go upward and build a stem, branches and leaves. The different parts of the plant are able—with the help of unicellular organisms—to combine water and minerals from the soil, carbon dioxide and oxygen from the atmosphere and energy from sunlight to produce and distribute nutriments to every cell of the plant. The tree is able to take advantage of three different media for its growth, reproduction and colonization of the environment. Such a diversification of functions is not characteristic of unicellular organisms.

In some multicellular species, their individuals associate and give rise to societies, organizations or communities. In these, members or individuals work for the wellbeing of themselves and the success of the species. They are societies that have developed a set of precise duties and rights that are enforced with decision. For each member of these species it would be difficult or impossible to subsist outside a society or to create a new one. Well-known examples of these species are bees, wasps, termites and *Homo sapiens*.

Because of its importance I have to set apart an example of organization of higher rank that includes all species of living beings, together with inorganic environments and natural phenomena that support them. Each species and each phenomenon are needed for the whole to subsist as such or for it to evolve and adapt to changes within a region or the planet. The study of an organization of this type is the object of Ecology as a science. In such an organization each component depends on all others. Species that are part of it increase or decrease their members as an adaptation to changes. Other possibilities include evolution or extinction.

In the case of man on Earth a unique phenomenon has occurred, by way of which he is able to compete in speed with the rest of natural processes in the physical and compositional transformation of the Earth's surface and atmosphere. This has been achieved without evolving into a new species, but by accumulation of knowledge. The distribution and use of this knowledge allowed man to advance to the status of dominant species. However, man continues to depend on the environment, which he only partially influences. The human species has been increasing the number of members through known history. This is a confirmation of its success. At the same time, with the great increase of his mobility, the species could be more at risk because of epidemics of different origins, such as those that are caused by mosquitoes, certain bacteria and other agents (Fauci and Morens, 2016).

CURRENT SOCIAL SITUATION OF HUMANITY

*"We pass through this world but once.
Few tragedies can be more extensive
than the stunting of life, few injustices
deeper than the denial of an
opportunity to strive or even to hope,
by a limit imposed from without, but
falsely identified as lying within."*
Stephen Jay Gould

Introduction

The geologic history of the Earth does not record any other species to have been as dominant as *Homo sapiens* are today. Man has reached such a position because of his unique success in searching for improvement of his condition. Such success is probably due to his curiosity, his power of observation, his power of interpretation, his capacity to communicate and, specially, his ability to accumulate and store information using artifacts not attached to his body. It is the use of writing in its different forms: Petroglyphs, papyruses, books, magnetic tapes, compact and hard discs and other devices and technologies.

With the aid of these technologies, man has reached the capacity to accumulate and transfer energy from several sources and to use it to extract, move, modify and use quantities of materials of the same order of magnitude that the Earth does through its natural processes. That is to say, building activities associated to roads, airports, cities, dams, canals, islands, and to extraction and use of industrial materials such as sand, limestone, coal, crude oil, and iron ore, are comparable, in terms of volume or mass, with the amounts of the erosion and transportation of materials that are not associated with man's activities (Peduzzi, 2014). This fact means that man shares with mother-nature the responsibility of determining or managing environmental conditions of the Earth's surface, the composition or distribution of sediments and waters of oceans, rivers and lakes, and the composition of the atmosphere.

Man's controlling power is accompanied by some positive interventions, and others not so positive. The power to change conditions of the Earth's surface includes the direct responsibility in the preservation of environments that allow the life of the rest of living beings that inhabit the planet (Calas, 2017).

It is known that all existing species are the result of a set of constantly-adjusting equilibria that are established through relationships among them and the environment. In some cases, those relationships have been studied; in other cases, they are unknown or involve species that have not yet been discovered by science. It is man's responsibility to monitor the existing equilibria and to prevent the introduction of perturbations that may cause disasters for many species, including his own.

Human societies have an almost global distribution. They add up to about 7,600 million members. They are administratively divided into 196 countries and 10 dependent territories. Countries are of very different sizes. A 36 per cent of the population belongs to 2 countries, and 50 per cent to 6 of them.

Many of these countries, particularly those with larger populations and territories, have separate internal societies, sometimes called nations, that are determined by ethnicity, religion, customs, language or traditions (China and India, for example). These societies have common laws but, in certain countries, may be governed using special laws, as it is the case with Iran and others.

In order to analyze and evaluate the most common social situations, it is useful to study governments that serve the people of the different countries, and take into account recommendations, suggestions and requirements of the organization to which the majority of them belong. That organization is the United Nations (UN).

Although the UN does not prescribe a specific government type, it has proposed the democratic governance as the seat of a group of values and principles that should be followed in order to reach social stability, citizens' participation, equity, security and human development.

Starting with the Declaration of Human Rights(1948) (http://www.un.org/en/universal-declaration-human-rights/), followed by the International Covenant on Civil and Political Rights (UNohchr, 1976), Essential Elements of Democracy (Meyer-Resende, 2011) and the Guidance Note of the Secretary-General on Democracy (UN, 2007), it has been established that democracy, based on the rule of law, is a way to achieve international peace and security, progress, economic, social and cultural development, and compliance with human rights.

Human rights fostered by the UN may be summarized as: 1. The *will of the people* is the basis on which the Government's authority rests; 2. Basic and irrevocable liberties are: Expression, peaceful meeting or association with other people; 3. Direct access to power or through representatives freely chosen, according to the rule of law; 4. Free, periodic and fair elections, with universal and secret votes, *as **the** expression of people's will*; 5. A plural system of political parties and political organizations; 6. Separation of powers; 7. Independence and stability of Judicial Power; 8. Responsibility and transparency in public administration; 9. Equal rights for men and women; and 10. Absence of discrimination based on race, genre, language, religion or other characteristics.

Because each individual or collective right is accompanied by a duty or several duties, it should be pointed out here that the UN has not been as diligent in the specifications of duties as it has been with human rights, exception made for tax contribution. As an example, the UN could have considered and approved the individual and collective duty of citizens to inform or claim government if a policy should not be working properly or causing damage. To that end, it should suggest institutional ways to comply. A *popular, public and peaceful demonstration* to complain an inconvenient government policy does not have the same importance nor the same power as the fulfillment of a citizen's legal duty—related to the same matter—done in a formal and reasoned manner through institutional channels. In the first case, it may well be interpreted as a disorderly bunch of people disturbing the peace; while in the second case, it has to be considered as an action that complies with the rule of law. This lack of precision or clarity or intention is probably due to the fact that the direct representatives of countries in the UN are their governments and, only rather indirectly, by the citizens of those countries. Governments do not necessarily favor citizens' duties that aid them to point out their shortcomings. Such duties would not be considered an innovation; they were part of democracy in ancient Greece (Aristotle, 2013).

Indices

In modern times the need to determine and compare the level of fulfillment of human rights in the different countries has fostered the generation and the improvement of a series of methods and indices for the task. Not only do these allow the comparison between countries but serve as a guide or as an alert for any government. A prominent group of indices, which are regularly published, follows.

The **Democracy Index** was developed by the Economist Intelligence Unit of the British newspaper The Economist (EIU). It evaluates the state of affairs of democracies for 165 nations and 2 territories, which covers most of the world's population. The index is based on data obtained by observing five areas: 1. Electoral process and pluralism; 2. Civil liberties; 3. Functioning of government; 4. Political participation; and 5. Political culture.

Table 1. Distribution, for the year of 2014, of the government types in 165 countries. They contain most of the world's population. (http://www.sudestada.com.uy/Content/Articles/421a3 13a-d58f-462e-9b24-2504a37f6b56/Democracy-index-2014.pdf)

Government Type	Number of Countries	Percentage of Countries	World's Population
Full Democracy	24	14.4	12. 5 %
Flawed Democracy	52	31.1	35.5 %
Hybrid Regime	39	23.4	14.4 %
Autocratic Regime	52	31.1	37.6 %

The collected data allow the classification of countries into the following groups as: a. Full democracies; b. Flawed democracies; c. Hybrid regimes; and d. Autocratic regimes.

The EIU publishes yearly the Democratic Index report. It includes collection-of-information methods, quantitative data for each country, regional and global tendencies, and interpretations of the cause-effect type. Table 1 (p. 28) summarizes the state of democratic development in the world for the year 2014.

It should be appreciated that more than half of the human population is being governed by governments that are not democratic. This situation is relevant to approximately 3,900 million people. According to the democratic index, only 12.5 per cent of the world's population can enjoy the protection of the complete set of human rights accorded by their country through the UN. It is a sad situation of great proportions.

The **Democracy Ranking** (DR) is published by the Democracy Ranking Association, whose seat is in Vienna, Austria. The DR lists only those countries that have been recognized as free or partially free by the Freedom House organization, and whose population is more than one million. In order to determine the quality of a democracy, it takes liberty into consideration with other characteristics of the political system, such as its performance in nonpolitical matters. These last ones are: genre, economy, knowledge, health, and environment. The index is published annually, accompanied by variations it has experienced through the years (http://democracyranking.org/wordpress/welcome/mission-statement/).

Freedom House is an organization whose purpose is to defend human rights. It does so by fostering liberty and democracy anywhere. It promotes studying obstacles to the achievement of liberty, advocates for more political rights and civil liberties, and gives support to their defenders. It is an American institution; it promotes leadership of United States of America, works with other nations that oppose dictatorship and oppression, and fosters changes toward democracy, with emphasis on political rights and civil liberties. It was founded 77 years ago, has its seat in the USA and it is not associated with political parties. It is described, perhaps incorrectly, as a nongovernmental organization (NGO), financed by the government of the USA and by entities and individuals of several countries.

Freedom House publishes yearly reports that cover several areas. These are: 1. Liberty in the world; 2. Freedom of the press; 3. Free access to the Internet; 4. Nations in transformation; 5. Countries at crossroads; and 6. Rights of women in the Middle East and North Africa. For each area mentioned, countries are classified into three or four categories. Generally, the yearly report includes a section for each country and deals with observed global tendencies. Table 2 (p. 31) gives quantitative data for the global overall situation for the year 2015.

Table 2. Distribution of the global population according to the quality of their liberty for year 2015. (https://freedomhouse.org/report/freedom-world/freedom-world-2016).

Quality of Liberty	World Population
Free	40 %
Partially Free	24%
Not Free	36 %

Human Rights Watch (HRW) is an independent organization, not associated with governments, that receives contributions or donations from individuals and foundations from all over the world. It does not accept funds, directly or indirectly, from any government. Its purpose is the defense of a complete spectrum of human rights and its coverage is global. The work within HRW is done by specialized professionals in human rights. They strive to establish facts, let them be known, and exert pressure directed to correct the undesirable conditions they have found.

HRW publishes, in many languages, yearly reports for each country. Each country's report describes its general situation, accompanied with the outstanding news for the year covered. No comparisons between countries are attempted; ranks or categories are not established. Reports are based on facts that are used to detect, describe and denounce the breach of human rights. Yearly, HRW also publishes its financial report regarding its administration. They can be found at: (https://www.hrw.org/).

One of the variables that influences the social environment of humans is corruption. It has a direct or indirect effect on a large portion of economic, cultural, educational, institutional, social, and personal activities. Due to this fact it has been the target for studies and comparisons by the United Nations (UN), Transparency International (TI), World Bank (WB), universities, think tanks, intern-governmental organizations etc. A list of these organizations can be found at the following website: (https://riacs.newark.rutgers.edu/intergovernmental-organizations).

TI evaluates how corruption in the public sector of countries is perceived. The corruption index that TI has developed has served to send a clear message to every country, so that it may be compelled to learn about its corruption and, perhaps, to act. This corruption index is well known. For the year of 2015 TI has estimated that more that 6,000 million people of 68 countries are suffering the effects of a serious corruption problem. These many people represent about 80 per cent of the world's population!

TI publishes yearly reports that include a world map that allows a quick visualization of the degree of corruption for each country. Reports contain a quantitative evaluation and the rank of the 168 countries— number 1 is the least corrupt. Variation of tendencies through time at the global, regional and country levels are included. The main causes for corruption in each case are highlighted (Transparency International, 2016).

The right to life and to personal security is an important factor to be considered in the evaluation of social situations. Internationally, the homicide rate, expressed as the number of culpable homicides for each 100,000 inhabitants per year, is the most complete, comparable and precise indicator for the measurement of violence; which, in turn, reflects personal insecurity or danger in a society.

Table 3. Number of culpable homicides in the different regions of the world for year 2012. Taken from the UN study on the subject (UNODC, 2013a).

Region	Homicides
Americas	157.000
Africa	135.000
Asia	122.000
Europe	22.000
Oceania	1.100
Total	437.100

The Global Study on Homicides 2013 by UNODOC (UN Office Against Drugs and Crime) presents and interprets data on homicides for 219 countries and territories. The report describes the situation of this phenomenon. It presents the main types of situations in which homicides occur. These are: 1. Socio-political; 2. Organized crime; and 3. Interpersonal relationships. It considers regions and countries where homicides take place more frequently. Identifies which parts of the population are more closely associated with homicides, as victims and as authors of crimes. Establishes the relationships between homicide rates with: 1. Laws and the rule of law; 2. Strategies and public policies; and 3. Uncertainty and fear that homicides cause to the population. Table 3 (p. 33) shows the magnitudes of culpable homicides for regions considered in the report.

A clear indicator of the current human social situation is the perception held by the people of different countries of their government and its most important divisions or components. Such perception may be quantified through the approval or disapproval of their performance. It is a reflection of the political knowledge of the population and the political history of the country, which may be measured on different occasions through time. The results of surveys that measure the approval of a government or some of its parts may not be amenable to an easy or direct interpretation. They depend on how the government has performed recently (improved or worsened); the direction or the policies that it has chosen (seems to be going in the right direction or not); who is preparing the surveys and who pays for them; which questions are chosen and which are avoided, towards whom they are directed and what is their purpose; the presence or absence of visible political alternatives; the freedom of expression that citizens can exert without fearing possible retaliation; and the people's knowledge of their rights and obligations.

It is expected that a population that knows its rights and duties should be more exacting towards its government than one that is not able to clearly identify its deficiencies. It also should be expected that a population which has been subjected by inefficient or totalitarian governments for a long time, at the arrival of one that is more efficient and allows more liberties, would likely express a higher approval than a population that recently has not experienced a notable change.

Table 4. Citizens' approval of their government, for a group of countries, measured on the dates shown. The data belong to governments as units and to some their parts. Data are taken from several public and free sources through the Web.

Country	Government or Component	Date	Approval (%)
Argentina	President	6/2016	44
Bangladesh	Government	2013	33
	Right Direction	2015	62
	Right Direction	2015	66
	Right Direction	2016	73
Brazil	President	10/2016	14
Canada	Prime Minister	9/2016	75
	Prime Minister	12/2016	55
China	Government	2013	85
Finland	President	2014	67
	Parliament	2014	25
	Government	2014	20
France	President	4/2016	12
Germany	Chancellor	4/2015	75
	Chancellor	2016	45
	Chancellor	6/2017	49
Greece	Government	2015	45
India	Prime Minister	2015	74
Indonesia	President	2016	67
Japan	Executive Power	2016	55
Mexico	President	2014	51
	President	2015	44
	The Military	2015	61

	Government	2015	27
Mongolia	President	2016	21
	Prime Minister	2016	24
	Wrong Direction	2916	19
	Supreme Court	2016	45
	Political Parties	2016	24
Nigeria	President	2016	44
Pakistán	Government	2011	28
	Judicial Power	2011	60
	The Military	2011	80
United Kingdom	Government	2015	38
Russia	President	12/2016	87
Russia	Right Direction	2/2016	45
Sweden	Government Coalition	2015	48
South Africa	President	3/2015	43
	President	4/2016	27
Tanzania	President	9/2016	88
United States	President	2/2017	45
	President	6/2017	39
	Congress	2016	13
	Congress	1/2017	19
Venezuela	President	5/2016	20
	President	5/2017	21
	National Assembly	5/2016	75
			X=46,3
			n=47

Data shown in Table 4 allow for the following observations: 1. Many government-approval values and those of important offices or units fall below fifty per cent; 2. Approval percentages may vary considerably in a short time (see data for the Chancellor of Germany, the Prime Minister of Canada and the President of Mexico); 3. Several governments have low approvals while their components fare better (see Finland, Mexico and Pakistan); 4. The average rate of approval for governments as a whole (n=8), is 44 per cent, while the average of all the approval data (n=47), is 46.3 per cent—values that are close to each other and support a general state of affairs; and 5. Some approval values seem to be abnormally high and should be studied, in order to discover the good behaviors that effectively induce people's approval (see Germany's Chancellor for 4/2015, governments of Bangladesh and China, presidents of Finland, Russia and Tanzania, and Prime Minister of India).

Following up on the mentioned cases of high approval, explanations for some of them have been found. Germany's chancellor, in few months, went from a 75 per cent approval to a 45 per cent, because she fostered economic and immigration policies that the people considered injurious and because she did not consider correcting them promptly.

The government of Bangladesh, a very poor country, achieved an approval of 66 per cent, not due to favorable conditions, but because the people felt that it *was on the right path* and wished it to continue.

China's government has traditionally obtained an approval of 85 per cent or more. This case has been studied in detail, especially because the country has endured important anti-government demonstrations on several occasions. Tang, Lewis-Becky and Martin (2013) concluded that the Chinese government is very careful and diligent in responding to complaints, requests and suggestions posed by the population, as long as the necessary arrangements do not endanger the government structure (Qian and Huo, 2017). The majority of the people feel they have been taken care of; the other 15 per cent thinks otherwise.

Tanzania's president received an 88 per cent approval. It is thought that such a distinction is due to the elimination of government "phantom" jobs, the establishment of a free educational system and the firing of corrupt employees (Mitulya, 2016).

Table 4 (p. 35) does not include the approval data of the twelve governments least approved by their citizens, for the year of 2014 (Hess and Frohlich, 2014). These are: 1. Bosnia-Herzegovina (8% approval); 2. Bulgaria (13%); 3. Greece (14%); 4. Czech Republic (15%); 5. Moldavia (18%); 6. Pakistan (18%); 7. Peru (18%); 8. Romania (18%); 9. Costa Rica (20%); 10. Jamaica (20%); 11. Portugal (20%); and 12. Spain (20%).

Even by taking into account that citizens' approval data depend on each country's specific conditions and some characteristics of the surveys used, I consider indisputable to conclude that, as a whole, they demonstrate that ***more than half of the human population withstands or tolerates a government that it does not approve***. Such state of affairs indicates a basic instability, whose fundamental causes are in urgent need of study and repair.

Another way to evaluate the social situation of a country or humanity as a whole is to determine how happy people feel. As an example, it may be that, for individuals, happiness could depend very little on government performance or, on the other hand, that such performance is very influential. Although happiness is not formally considered a human right by the UN, the organization has been giving it increasing attention.

The first UN World Happiness Report was published in 2012 and was followed by yearly reports. The last report is the World Happiness Report 2016, Update Volume I (Helliwell et al., 2016). The need to quantify happiness has prompted the development of new measuring methods and the incorporation of results from psychological, social and neurological research related to its surrogate, the subjective wellbeing (Pasquali, 2014a, p. 105-110).

Happiness is considered as the best indication of social progress and achievement of goals of social policies. The **Happiness Index** developed by the UN, to be applied to countries, is determined by six variables: 1. Gross domestic product per capita; 2. Social support (to have someone that can help in case of difficulties); 3. At birth, the number of years of an expected healthy life; 4. Freedom to make one's life choices; 5. Generosity measured by donations recently made; and 6. Trust measured as absence of corruption. The resulting index is expressed by a number on a 1 to 10 scale. Countries are ranked from 1 to 157, from a high degree of happiness to the most severe misery (Helliwell et al., 2016).

It has been found that wellbeing inequality perceived by citizens in their society is a better indication of happiness than their income or wealth. At the same time, the creation of organizations, where people get together regularly to socialize and show mutual support, in a respectful environment of secular ethics, is highly recommended. These organizations would have the purpose to inspire and unite people of all cultures in harmony with the main religions (Layard in Helliwell et al., 2016).

Because of its importance, to conclude this section, the following expression of Human Right Watch in 2015 is highlighted here (HRW, 2015): ***"Changes in the democratic mechanisms to allow for the expression of human capacities are recommended. Complete participation is achieved when citizens are given the opportunity to contribute to the deliberation process."*** This matter will be dealt with in detail in the following chapters.

General View

There is no *one* social human condition or situation. What is observed is a multitude of them, which are determined by combinations of circumstances and sub-environments. The main ones are: 1. Genetic characteristics of individuals; 2. Family; 3. Community or neighborhood; 4. City; 5. State, region or tribe; 6. Country; and 7. Earth. Each of these environments or variables exerts influence of a different nature on the individual during his life time. At the same time, each person has a corresponding effect on others in his or her surroundings.

Analyzing circumstances and sub-environments mentioned above it becomes obvious that, with the exception of genetic characteristics and Earth, government has a very important, if not decisive, influence on man's condition in his society. In the next chapter *Individual Development* those variables that are closely associated with expected government's responsibilities are analyzed in detail.

This author has concluded that most humans sustain the *general perception* that, there is a need and a possibility to get much closer to a state where the individual is able to enjoy those rights that are considered inherent to human nature, and which many governments have recognized but not fulfilled.

Citizens should search for answers to questions such as: Why is it that such a *general perception* does not originate profound government changes? Could it be an indication of a structural problem, in government systems as we now know them, which will not allow better performances?

The measurement of government characteristics through the indices—democracy, quality of liberty, protection of human rights, corruption, right to life and personal security, approval and happiness—paints a desperate situation. More than half of governments are not democratic. Only in 40 per cent of countries the liberty of citizens is considered acceptable. The government type with more population is the Autocratic Regime —with 37.6 per cent of the total.

Human rights, although in different degrees, are not respected in the majority of nations. The most serious problems are: 1. Government oppression, destruction of the civil society, and the fear created within the population; 2. Restriction to information available through the Web, due to the effect it may produce on political movements; 3. Low citizen participation in government affairs; 4. High numbers of children from adolescent mothers; 5. Discrimination based on ethnicity, political ideologies or preferences, economic means, status, etc.; 6. Generalized corruption; 7. Religious intolerance; 8. Differences in purposes of governments; and 9. Hypocrisy employed as a political tool.

The perceived general view may be seen in different ways. One of them is to simply *contemplate* things as they are, with the sufferings they produce, and live with the idea that time will take care of things or avoid thinking about it. A different way is to face the facts, analyze and interpret them, create corrective plans and exert pressure to get them executed.

The remainder of the book is dedicated to that end.

INDIVIDUAL DEVELOPMENT

"Each new generation is in effect an invasion of civilization by little barbarians, who must be civilized before it is too late."
Thomas Sowell

"Society exists for the benefit of its members, not the members for the benefit of society."
Herbert Spencer

"Early childhood education is the key to the betterment of society."
Maria Montessori

Introduction

The study of society starts with the study of its members, from conception to death. In this chapter an attempt is made to examine the most important factors that determine behavior, wellbeing and happiness of the people. Also, how these factors may help shape the government they will choose or tolerate.

Factors of different natures are recognized: Congenital, social (family, close ambience or group, nation, country and global), psychologic, economic; environmental and related to health. In most situations these factors do not act in isolation. Their final effect, on an individual or on a group, depends on a combination of them, which makes it difficult to evaluate quantitatively their separate contributions. Emphasis is made here on those aspects that represent an opportunity to better society by changing government structures, responsibilities and activities which promote positive personal behaviors.

Humans live in societies because of the advantages they represent or offer. There will always be a constant competition, evaluation or confrontation between the advantages of social life or life in a society, and the limitations and sacrifices that social life imposes on the individual. This competition is derived from an unstable or meta-stable equilibrium that depends on circumstances and the state of development of each society. This means that the missions or responsibilities that should be assigned to any government change with time. These missions should include the contribution to the solution of current problems that citizens are not able to solve on their own. At the same time, government should earn and receive the collective support of citizens.

For example, a society where citizens have a personal or family income that covers their common needs, should not require that government—with the funds that are contributed by the whole population—initiate or sustain a program to aid personal income. If the same society is suffering a drug-use problem, it would require from government the creation of a system capable of diminishing the use of drugs, deal with its consequences and help treat those that have become victims of it.

A poor society, where most people do not have a personal or family income sufficient to cover the cost of basic needs, represents another example, and a much more serious problem. In this case, citizens should require from government the promotion of a more productive allocation of existing natural, human, manufactured, social and financial capital. Urgent and consistent emphasis should be put on increasing human capital and into protecting existing financial capital, by fighting corruption with firmness of purpose. To achieve positive and lasting results does not necessarily require the direct input of government funds; perhaps it may only require the protection of private property, the approval of appropriate laws and the guarantee of compliance with them (Boragina, 2016; and references therein).

In any case, societies should be governed by making use of policies that include modern knowledge in a variety of disciplines and, at the same time, opinions and feelings of their members.

Genesis

Many think that the genotype—the sum of the genetic material transmitted through parents—is what determines capacities, inclinations, health and life. That is not so. As an example, in humans, the risk caused by the genetic factor on the probability to develop most illnesses has been estimated to be between 10 and 20 per cent (Greger and Stone, 2015; Greger y Stone, 2016). Genes do not determine diseases; genes, either good or bad, only work when activated or able to express themselves. The diet composition, for example, plays a key role in the determination of which genes may be active in the majority of cases (Campbell and Campbell, 2006; Campbell and Campbell, 2012).

The literature indicates that circumstances involved in the formation of human beings begin before conception. The woman's age, her mental and physical health, her economic status and her education, and the same properties of her spouse, plus the quality of the relationship between them, are found to be important factors in the determination of a pregnancy free of somatic or psychological complications.

The risk factors related to bad mental health during pregnancy include a record of family psychological illnesses, the use of drugs, a past of disorderly sexual conduct, physical or emotional abuse, current social adversity or relevant events during this period. Factors that contribute to anxiety and depression during pregnancy vary greatly among countries. The most commonly mentioned are: lack of support from the spouse, poverty, a numerous progeny, a low educational level of the husband, and the lack of a person in which to trust her problems. It has been found that depression of the mother in the postnatal period interferes with the development of the baby; lowers cognitive development and physical growth (Black et al., 2017; Britto et al., 2017; Richter et al., 2017).

A critical factor in the development of children is nutrition. In the words of Grantham-McGregor et al. (1999): *"There is now a large and increasing body of evidence to indicate that nutrition and health affect children's cognitive, motor, and behavioral development, both pre- and postnatally."* When relating child development with the social environment, evidence supports that inequities in development begin prior to conception, and that timely interventions reduce inequities and increase productivity (Georgiadis and Penny, 2017).

A matter of special importance has to do with the adolescent mother. She may have married very young, not be married and have a stable partner or have no partner. Each one of these circumstances has social, economic and health consequences for the future of the mother and that of her children. Pregnancy at an early age is accompanied by disadvantages for the mother's physical and educational development and that of her baby.

Especially the youngest and poorest mothers statistically ingest an inferior diet, receive inadequate medical care and are assigned harder tasks. Frequently they suffer violence and abuse from their surroundings. If that were not bad enough, young mothers that have suffered abuse tend to turn into abusers that create an inter-generational continuity of their condition.

Do you not agree that this type of information should reach, at the right time, in detail, all young people of your country? The educational system of a country could help with this task. However, adults in the family may be in a better position to deliver such information, at the proper time, with perseverance and effectiveness.

Family

The family is an important social value, not only for children and adults, but also for their society. Traditionally the family was composed of a man, a woman and their children, although other arrangements were known. The development of modern societies has allowed or fostered the frequent development of other structures that comply with similar functions to those of the traditional family.

It may be of use to mention those functions that are generally expected from a traditional family, just as they are from their substitutes, as far as they are germane to children. Children have the right to receive support from their family and their community, to be protected from war and violence, to live a life free from adult sexuality and to be recognized as individuals and as members of a group (Garbarino, 1998).

The term *child* in this section refers to infants to 19-year-old youngsters. Although the care and treatment to which they are entitled change according to their age, so do their duties and responsibilities.

Family is understood to be a stable organization. In such family, parents or persons that take care of children are constant, consistent and maintain through time a close relationship with them, are mentally healthy, use adequate upbringing practices; maintain a coherent family system, and support a home environment that fosters and stimulates (Harden, 2004).

The reader may ask why so much detail on a subject as well known as the family. It turns out that the proper commitment of a family to its responsibilities produces excellent results for its members. On the other hand, its faulty operation not only produces terrible consequences for its members, especially for children, it is also one of the most important factors that aid the development of the *great evils* of societies. The knowledge of this causality, in turn, opens an opportunity to prevent the development of toxic families and to foster those that are healthy and stable. These will help repair their societies.

Toxic or risky families create an adverse social environment, with two general characteristics, conflict and aggression, and a cold, unsupportive or neglected home. The main consequences are: The creation of genetic vulnerability in offspring, which cause difficulties in processing and controlling emotions; unhealthy social behaviors, such as drug abuse, aggression and dropping out of school; and the increase of risk for mental disorders, chronic diseases, such as cancer, asthma, cardiovascular diseases and depression (Repetti et al., 2002).

The causes for the formation of toxic families are numerous. The most common are: 1. Poverty; 2. Unhealthy social environment; 3. Divorce; 4. Marriage involving adolescents; 5. Low educational level of parents; 6. Poor educational systems; and 7. Hard-to-bear social traditions.

On the basis of the nature of causes mentioned in the preceding paragraph, it can be concluded that the common phenomenon of the toxic family has deep roots. Risky families are found in many societies, they commonly establish a continuity of behavior that carries from one generation to the next, which makes for an intimidating forecast of what is to be expected for the future.

Regarding the first cause mentioned—poverty, also called low socioeconomic status—it is worth quoting an expression by Repetti et al. (2002, p. 359): *"The adverse effects of low socioeconomic status on mental and physical health are as close to a universal truth as a social science has offered. Without attention to the social contexts in which families develop, and in which risk and resilience are transmitted from generation to generation, scientists will remain the helpless chroniclers of the outcomes described in this article."*

The contents of this quote leave no doubt that poverty, in itself, is not a virtue, as some religions and governments predicate, insinuate or try to convince and acclaim. Much to the contrary, it is an unfortunate condition, full of deprivations for those that suffer it. One of the urgent duties of societies and governments is to foster the abatement and elimination of poverty.

Adolescent pregnancy is a phenomenon of developed countries just as of poor undeveloped ones. In the last ones, the socially acceptable age for the marriage of girls is the product of customs, traditions and religions. To illustrate, the age at which 50 per cent of Bangladesh women marry is 14.1 years, 15.1 years for Niger, 15.8 years for Yemen, 16.1 years for India, and 16.4 years for Senegal (WHO, 2004). Globally, the average rate of child birth by mothers between 15 and 19 years of age, which excludes those between 12 and 14 years of age and does not mention abortion rates, is 6.5 births per 1000 women. It is an indication that, deliveries by very young mothers constitutes an important factor to be considered when the health, wellbeing and security of societies are under consideration.

For children and adolescents that have suffered the effects of a toxic family or have no family at all, societies have attempted several ways to protect and guide them. One way has been the use of orphanages. Unfortunately, these highly formalized systems lead to the institutionalization of children, where they are exposed to dangerous environments that are full of obstacles for their good development (Goffman, 1961; Goffman, 2001; Harden, 2004; Juffer et al., 2017).

Community, Town, City and Country

After the family, neighborhood, town, city and nation are the entities that hold social capital. It is expected that the individual has access to all benefits derived from that capital. Among those benefits, the most important are: 1. Liberty for his development according to his wishes, inclination and capacities; 2. Creation of neighborhood environments for mutual support; 3. Access to a health system; 4. Sufficient knowledge or education needed to behave as a productive citizen in a modern society; 5. A set of habits and norms that encompass respect, collaboration, kindness, communication and a feeling of unity or belonging; 5. A national Constitution; 5. An ensemble of laws that, when upheld, aids a peaceful coexistence; 8. A childhood and a youth that are protected from problems of adults; 9. Direct personal participation in public matters; 10. The possibility to contribute to an increase of the human and social capital for coming generations; 11. Opportunities for work to support himself/herself and his/her family; and 12. A peaceful international environment based upon appropriate exchanges between nations.

Social capital has been mentioned. It may be useful to clarify the sense in which it is used here. Although capitals have been arranged in different sets, we will group them here into four types. These are: physical or natural capital, which includes money and material goods; human capital, which includes the formation of the individual, his culture and his education; environmental capital; and social capital. The last one, as all other types of capital, is an ingredient that fosters productivity because it allows the achievement of results that, without it, would not be possible. It may serve as a favorable or unfavorable ingredient for society. It is brought about through changes in the relations between people or organizations to make some actions easier. To set up a warning system for the protection of a neighborhood is increasing social capital, while to organize a group for the distribution and sale of drugs is increasing negative social capital. One way to visualize how social capital works is by analyzing how it influences the operation of a family.

The physical or financial capital of a family is its income and wealth; it may be expressed by a monetary value. The human capital of a family is composed mostly of the parent's education. In order for those two capitals to be used for the benefit of a family it is necessary that parents dedicate time and show affection to their children. The right disposition and the time dedicated are part of the social capital of the family. Without them, the wealth and knowledge of parents would be of little use to the wellbeing of children.

The most common social insufficiency of modern families is the presence of only one parent. In them, social capital is automatically diminished.

The effects of the social capital are especially important in the development of human capital for the next generation. Investment in physical and human capital creates advantages for its owners, while investment in social capital produces benefits for all members of the social structure (Coleman, 1988).

The analysis presented in the previous chapter *Current Social Situation of Humanity* indicates that, in actual practice, it is possible to effectively fulfill most citizens' aspirations related to the society in which they live. However, the present state of affairs indicates that most people are not receiving such benefits.

With the currently known government structures it has been impossible to prevent or effectively correct some traditional social problems. The main ones are: 1. The existence of marginal populations that suffer low income, violence, inadequate housing, unhealthy environments, lack of medical care and poor children's education; 2. A political environment that will not allow or makes it very difficult for the common citizen to have any meaningful effect on his government; 3. A high rate of child birth by very young mothers; 4. A high proportion of risky or toxic families; 5. Inequity of educational opportunities for children (Hudson and Kühner, 2016); 6. A disproportional influence of power groups; 7. An encroachment of organized crime; and 8. A health system that does not use modern research results (Horton, 2016a; Horton, 2016b; Horton, 2016c).

The Earth

The common environment for all humans is the Earth. From a global point of view this social setting may be examined through countries' characteristics. It is the ambient in which the UN acts. Through UN's and other organizations' data, suggestions, norms and binding agreements, it is possible to identify those nations whose governments foster or hamper the achievement of needs and aspirations of human beings. Within them, it is also possible to identify *circumstances, specific actions and policies* that lead to undesirable effects of great magnitude. These effects, perhaps, might be predicted early enough to prevent their development. Examples of some of these effects are colonization, large migratory movements, political, economic and technological dependences, rebellions, and wars.

The evolution of the global human society acquires an extraordinary opportunity with the advent of modern communication techniques. It is now possible to disseminate key knowledge for the appropriate development of the individual in all stages of life, very quickly and virtually at no cost.

These techniques may promote research and collaboration aimed at the improvement of those toxic environments that have been identified. They may also foster comparisons, exchange of results, protocols and applications that will increase the effectiveness of aid contributed by donors to help countries or groups in dire need.

Summary

The panorama that emerges from the study of the formation of the individual, attempted in this chapter, on the basis of the known environments where and when it takes place, is that such formation, in general terms, is a predictable product of the combination of multiple connected factors. Some of these factors are: genetic, instinctive, accidental, planned, young-age pregnancy, family support, social support, parents' age, social economic status, housing arrangements, health protection, parents' love, parents' time dedicated to children, number of brothers and sisters, critical years for adequate nutrition for development, quality of neighborhood, educational culture, formal education, opportunities for education, school environment, tragedy in the family, social tragedies, wars, friendships, desertion of children, conditions in an orphanage, quality of jobs, functionality of society, creation of a life plan, stability of family during old age, religious upbringing, comparisons with other countries and communication among citizens.

There are immeasurable numbers of possibilities in the formation of individuals. For each individual they are unique. Societies are built only of unique individuals; their characteristics and their quality, as related to the wellbeing of their members, depend greatly on their ability to increase and maintain their positive social, physical, human and environmental capitals.

At each point of their history, each nation finds itself with a unique combination of individuals and capitals. Each nation will increase, diminish or manage its total capital in different ways that depends considerably on decisions and actions under the control of its government and knowledge and decisions of its population. Future results will also depend on external factors.

Factors coming from surroundings may be very diverse and can only be dealt with by each specific nation at any given time. Examples of external factors could be: a powerful aggressive neighbor nation, limitations to import essential commodities, international agreements or treaties or historical events that endanger the control of the territory, a war declaration or invasion, a devastating earthquake or an epidemic of ample distribution.

Among internal factors two are of uppermost importance: 1. Family structure and functionality; and 2. Government system and structure.

Given the proven fact that *the development of every individual* depends on the circumstances in which he is conceived, the characteristics of his parents, the care and nutrition that he will receive, and the harmony and stability of the family group, it is essential that those conditions be as favorable as they may be, for the individual and, collectively, for his society. Since those conditions are, at least partially, under the control of the will-be parents, it is their personal obligation to be informed of their present and future responsibilities and their ability to comply, and to exert sexual responsibility to prevent limitations and suffering for their own offspring (Nhat Hanh, 1999).

Government, typically through a Constitution, coordinates basic policies which allow for the operation of society. Government also determines actions and conditions that will shape short, medium and long-term future.

In order to take the best available course of action, a government has to use all knowledge at its disposal. Within that knowledge, preferences of the current population and protection of coming generations stand out.

Information presented in the prior chapter *Current Social Situation of Humanity,* demonstrates that a substantial fraction of the world's population does not feel appropriately represented by their government or are not satisfied with its performance. At the same time, this fraction seems to discern with precision which governments offer the most favorable conditions for the wellbeing of its members and, on that basis, important migratory flows are established.

In the following chapters several government structures that favor a genuine citizenry's representation, an efficient operation and an evolution toward happier future generations are presented.

FAVORABLE STRUCTURES

"Knowing when to refocus from another viewpoint, and when to sacrifice a system that has begun to constrain expansion and expression, is a sign of mastership."
David Allen

"High-performance organizations have clear missions and are structured in such a way as to focus energy towards the achievement of those missions."
Susan M. Gates

Introduction

The structure of an organization is built to suit its functional effectiveness. This implies that its functions should be previously determined. For the case of companies that manufacture goods or offer services, with the basic purpose of producing benefits for their owners or shareholders and to comply with a social mission, the most common legal structure is widely known. Typically, it consists of an Assembly which represents the interests of shareholders or owners, holds the power of direction and decision and a Board of Directors, which executes the assembly's decisions through divisions, departments, sectors, etc. There are other legal arrangements that, depending on their selected missions and their social environments, have also been successful. Two of these are the cooperative or co-op and the credit union.

In the case of governments of nations there are many structures being used. They have not been built, necessarily, after finding out which are the missions that the people or the citizens expect will be the responsibility of their government. They could have been the result of historical events that are unrelated to agreements reached by the people. This means that it is probable that many such governments maintain structures that are not suitable for their society. Additionally, societies change naturally with time and the missions that are expected from them also change. Unfortunately, many of these obsolete government structures are not being challenged, in spite of inefficiency, waste and contradiction they generate with their operation. Experience has demonstrated that it is very difficult to change such structures (Klitgaard and Light, 2005).

It is conceivable that a considerable number of current nations have governments with structures that make them inefficient, because of their history or because of the evolution of their society. The fact that the majority of the world's population is not satisfied with their government's performance—see chapter *Current Social Situation of Humanity*—could be an indication that their structures are the cause or that they contribute to the maintenance of such a state of affairs.

From Needs to Missions

The determination of missions and responsibilities, with which government has to comply, is a key stage for any society. The natural procedure to determine such missions is to adjust them to the needs and preferences of citizens. The resulting set defines the government's purpose. The manner in which it is carried out and the level of participation of the citizenry in the process determine to a high degree the contents of the Constitution and the future social stability of the country. Each current government, typically, already has a long list of responsibilities, many of which may be inappropriate or inconsistent with the needs and preferences of the population. Here, arbitrarily, but with the aid of the literature and experience, a group of missions that are considered sovereign and essential is adopted. The intent is to illustrate a way to derive a structure that will aid the fulfillment of the purpose of a government of a well-balanced society (Knott and Miller, 1987; Gates, 2005, in Klitgaard and Light; Christensen et al., 2007).

Although the present adoption of government's responsibilities has been arbitrary, it represents what I have perceived are the missions or areas that are in need of urgent attention for many countries, as indicated by the types of news that are divulged daily. Consequently, these responsibilities could be useful to many countries. It does not matter if these should be equal, similar or different from those that are suitable to the citizens of the reader's country or society. To find out, in any case, which are those missions or areas that require a high governmental responsibility (MHGR), a method for their practical determination will be described in chapter *Inclusive Power*.

The chosen missions or MHGRs are: 1. **Personal liberty**. It includes the rule of law, life development, freedom of expression, association, economic activity, beliefs, and movement within and out of the country; 2. **Personal security.** It includes life protection, housing, food, work, armed forces and police; 3. **Health protection**. It includes a network for medical care, psychological and nutritional care, and instruction directed toward protection of pregnant women and young children; 4. **Environmental care**. It includes monitoring activities and toxic substances to man and other species, national parks of diverse types, and protection of flora, fauna and environment; 5. **National productivity**. It includes economic, cultural, spiritual and traditional production, the establishment and maintenance of infrastructures for energy, transportation and communication sectors; 5. **International relations**. It includes the country's legal representation in international settings, fostering scientific, cultural and environmental agreements, and aid and support to its citizens when in foreign lands; 7. **Education**. It includes an educational system that covers all levels— from kindergarten to doctoral degrees and covering scientific, technological, health, cultural and humanist areas—and a network for the dissemination and exchange of information; and 8. **Will of the People**.

It includes a system by which the collective and sovereign will of the people can be expressed at any time.

From Missions to Structure

In a similar way as the missions have to adjust to needs, government structures have to adjust to missions (MHGRs). Entities of higher rank within a government—ministries, state departments, divisions, as they may be called—should be determined by missions. Each of these entities should contain all agencies or institutions that have functions needed to achieve the mission's goals.

If a new set of MHGRs should be determined for a government, it would mean that its priorities have changed. Some entities of high rank, such as Ministries, will be created and some eliminated. The same will be true for entities of lower ranks. If their activities are no longer needed they will be eliminated; if they grow in importance they will increase in rank; and, if they diminish in importance they will decrease in rank. The procedure would be something like cleaning and organizing house, as required for the adoption and inclusion of *only* those specific missions that have been chosen. It could be referred to as one of the cures for government's obesity. Perhaps, it will also require changes in the relations among powers that would need to be specified in the Constitution. There would be compulsory collaboration between powers, but no duplication of responsibilities or functions.

For example, in the case of the arbitrarily-adopted missions, the Executive Power will include the Presidency or its equivalent. It will be accompanied by eight ministries that correspond to the eight missions selected—unless some of those eight missions are fulfilled by another Power. In each Ministry there will only be the essential employees needed for the development of policies that will ensure the attainment of their central objective and no other. Ministries will coordinate the actions of the agencies of the next lower administrative level. These will take care of the day-to-day activities within their specific responsibilities. They could be Directions, Institutes, Departments, etc., all of the same next lower administrative rank in relation to the Ministry.

This arrangement ensures that each government's mission serves as the name and area of responsibility of one and only one Ministry. It is its only purpose and reason to exist. It is well known that efficient organizations are those that have a clear mission, have no duplicity of functions, and reach excellence in what they do. In governments that have more Ministries than missions, tenacious resistance to their elimination or even the creation of new ones is to be expected.

That resistance must be defeated. If this is not done successfully, there will be organizations with activities that should be a part of a sequence, that are not controlled by those that have the responsibility to achieve a goal. Such a situation will be an obstacle to supervision, to smooth instructions flow, and will add to the total cost of operation.

Similar considerations, as related to chosen missions, should also take place in the Legislative and Judiciary Powers.

Experience shows that all structural changes to government will be tenaciously opposed. A viable way to introduce them is through the **Will of the People** that pertains to the society where such mission has been established or decided. This critical step will be considered in chapter *Inclusive Power* (p. 103).

The introduction of changes in the structure of a government, especially a democratic government, is a difficult task because the existing structure has been the product of complex piecemeal negotiations and consists of an unstable equilibrium between political leaders and organizations that opposed themselves through time (Klitgaard and Light, 2005; Gates in Klitgaard and Light). No political power wishes to relinquish earned positions. This is the main reason that structural changes that are proposed either are not achieved or achieved through very slow processes. This sluggishness is accompanied by an additional danger: It provides time that may be used by opponents to distort missions and prevent the desired increase in government's efficiency.

The formulation of a common purpose or general Will of the People has not been performed in a credible and socially inclusive way because of a lack, within the government structure of a practical system capable to collect and manage the needed information from all citizens that are willing to contribute. The system should be able to receive information, interpret it, transform it into proposals or alternatives and evaluate their separate citizens' support.

Probably, the major obstacle for the adoption of such a system is the lack of government's will to do so: It may turn out to be inconvenient for the preconceived ideas, postures and conveniences that most of those in power enjoy.

When a system with these properties is installed, the strength of the people's opinions and preferences can be used to modify the status quo decisively. That action would also indicate capacity to comply with the direct form of participation found in item (a) of article 25 of the International Covenant on Civil and Political Rights of the UN (UNohchr, 1976): *"To take part in the conduct of public affairs, directly or through freely chosen representatives."*

From Missions and Structure to System

To extract weighted opinions from the People is a communication process. Citizens have to establish communication among themselves, propose and choose those matters that are of interest, express their ideas, examine the ideas of others, revise their own, follow improvements achieved as exchanges of data and opinions take place, and give their support or rejection to those that are finally put up for final evaluation.

Traditional politicians would probably see with displeasure the implications of the existence of a process with these characteristics. It is expected that they will state that this imbroglio is unnecessary; citizens give their opinions with their vote at elections of the different types. What they would probably not mention is that to vote is not the same as to give a *free* personal opinion, it consists only in the selection, among options determined or permitted by others, the one that he/she considers more convenient or the one that he/she dislikes the least. There is no free opinion in a vote: It is confined, funneled and forced. It does take into account neither candidates nor ideas which the voter may consider superior to those proposed on the ballot. From this viewpoint one may think of elections as a method that has been designed to *exclude the direct opinion* of citizens.

The possibility of establishing a constant and effective communication among millions of individuals was not possible until a few decades ago. It came to be with the development of Internet. Currently there exist a variety of programs, many of which are in the public domain, that may be used or adapted to a system that comply with the characteristics required by a communication project such as has been presented.

An operational condition of the Project is that the *information has to come from each separate individual, since it is the unit from which People are built, and it is the atomized political power.* In any given country, it is only necessary that the individual belong to an administrative political division of the nation: State, county, city, municipality, parish, etc. In such a fashion that, within the same system, different sub-societies with different problems, opportunities and number of members can discuss their issues. Any given individual should be able to interact on matters related to his municipality, city, state and country.

It could turn out to be a discussion point if it would be convenient or constructive that, on any or some matters, individuals not belonging to a specific administrative division, where a problem is being treated, would be allowed to give an opinion or contribute information and, if so, under what conditions. In any case, such individuals should not have the right to support or reject an idea or action, when it is being evaluated for administrative or legal procedures.

Just as organizations do not have the right to vote, as such, in elections where citizen vote as individuals, they should not have the right to participate, opine and evaluate *as organizations.* That right is exclusive for *individual citizens* that are members of a political administrative division.

To establish a smooth operation of such a system in a country may require several months for installation, testing, instruction and practice. It implies the access to the Web by the majority of the population, through personal computers, public library facilities and, perhaps, municipal offices. Every citizen can enroll in the system, choose a login password and indicate his administrative division. The system's administrator must verify that the data provided are correct in order to determine the individual's right to evaluate quantitatively the political strength of ideas or actions that result from the online discussions.

After having ensured the funds for the development and installation of the system, I estimate that it could be producing useful results a year later (see p. 152). Sometime ago I searched for possible private sources that might be interested in funding the initial phase of such a system. These have been discussed elsewhere (Pasquali, 2014b).

A contribution to a clear appreciation of the toxic causes and consequences that members of society have to endure because of unsuitable government structures are presented in the next chapter *Political Toxicology*.

POLITICAL TOXICOLOGY

Can you imagine hearing a newly elected official taking the following oath of office: *"Do you solemnly swear that if you are not here to help us you at least won't hurt us?"*
Dr. McKinley Johnson

"It is no measure of health to be well adjusted to a profoundly sick society."
Jiddu Krishnamurti

"When the fabric of society is so rigid that that it cannot change quickly enough, adjustments are achieved by social unrest and revolutions."
John Boyd Orr

"I am acutely conscious of the advantages of democracy over dictatorship. But the superiority of democracy over other forms of government leaves open the possibility that democracy might function better if its powers were more tightly limited."
Ilya Somin

Introduction

This chapter deals with the symptoms of troublesome operation that government and society commonly show. It includes discussions and illustrations of behavior of politicians, political representation of citizens, communication among citizens, populations' political knowledge and governmental changes of structure.

Symptoms Related to Government

Indicators that a government is not operating well are numerous and varied. A group of these follows. The presence of a combination of several of them is evidence for a complex situation that requires a holistic solution.

The selected indicators are: 1. Extensive discretion granted to public officials; 2. Fear of the population of the police, the military and secret service; 3. Legislation that hinders or does not allow the free expression of citizens; 4. Obstacles to the free access to information; 5. Limitations to travel within the country or to leave it and return; 6. Ostentatious presence of armed officials in public places; 7. Lack of celerity or quality of services offered by government; 8. Disrespect for the environment; 9. Lack of maintenance and hygiene of public places; 10. Disregard for the rule of law; 11. Disregard for modern knowledge while taking decisions; 12. Poor relationships of government with institutions of learning; and 13. Government's low regard for opinions and complaints expressed by citizens.

Fortunately, basic conditions or causes that give raise to a faulty government operation are few and are related to each other. They also have much in common with those toxic causes that determine a troublesome operation of society. This being the case, political changes that are expected to improve government and society are treated jointly.

Symptoms Related to Societies

Symptoms that society is malfunctioning are conditions that have an effect on a large number of people, hinder the achievement of a healthy life for the population or endanger the stability of society itself. The presence of several of these symptoms, if not dealt with, may mean that such a society is not viable.

Some of these symptoms are: 1. Poverty that jeopardizes health and capacity for work; 2. Insecurity for the life of individuals and their properties; 3. Large migration of individuals to other countries or from other countries; 4. Lack of individual liberty to choose goals or a way of life; 5. Weakness of the family structure, specially a high frequency of adolescent mothers; 6. Shortage of high-quality educational opportunities that foster the increase of human capital and adequate remunerations for a healthy life; 7. Strong presence of organized crime; 8. Lack of agreement or harmony between ethnic, religious, political and cultural groups or sectors of society; and 9. Improper use of material, human, social and environmental capital available to society.

While all symptoms seem to be present, in different degrees, in all societies, their consequences do not necessarily develop in all countries. For each reader it will be very easy to diagnose if his country suffers a specific toxic situation, because it is not a matter that can be hidden.

Improper Behavior by Politicians

Politics takes place more frequently and intensely through or among politicians. A brief incursion into what has been published on the psychology of politicians as a group may help to understand their behavior. *Politician* has many meanings. Here it is used as a noun that indicates a person, man or woman, which studies, researches or takes part in State matters or businesses. Three main types of politicians are recognized: 1. The academician or studious person dedicated to political sciences; 2. A government official that develops or carries into effect policies in any area; and 3. A person that, may or may not be a member of a political party, but that earns a government post through an election by citizens. Types 2 and 3 are considered below.

Political psychology has recorded that a considerable number of politicians belongs to six personality types: Narcissistic, obsessive-compulsive, Machiavellian, authoritarian, paranoiac and totalitarian. The most common are the narcissistic and the obsessive-compulsive; the first being the most frequent (Cohen, 2011; Rosen, 2013).

Most politicians have narcissistic tendencies; they feel they are entitled to power to influence the lives of others. They are known for their desire for admiration and greatness, demand loyalty, and are exploiters, very convincing liars and good leaders.

Obsessive-compulsive politicians are hard workers, conscientious and ethical. They shine through their achievements and capacities, although not through their personalities. They are excellent in the design of policies, defend the status quo and are seldom good leaders.

Machiavellians are skilled manipulators that use people's interests and weaknesses for their political and personal benefit. They are calm and calculating individuals that do not suffer from ethical impediments while achieving their objectives. Victory is all, the rest is negotiable.

Authoritarians—should not be confused with members of authoritarian regimes or authoritarian beliefs—are eminently hierarchical. They flatter their bosses, compete with those of the same rank and are dominant toward their subordinates. They appreciate courage and strength, while despising mercy and compassion. Are typically conservatives, retain prejudices for long periods and love rules.

Paranoiacs are reserved and suspicious, hold doubts about the loyalty of people around them, and frequently hold resentments for a long time. It is thought that this personality is a compensation caused by feelings of inferiority mixed with rage and resentment.

Totalitarians are rather rare in politics that take place in systems that employ elections. They associate themselves with strong and arbitrary governments. They distinguish themselves by their cult of personality and the belief in the leader's infallibility.

It is interesting to know the probable *intention* that the politician may have in his professional performance. To develop this subject matter, I include ideas taken from the literature that may help to visualize intentions in three groups of people within a democratic country. Other government types have similar groups, although their relative power may be different.

The notable American writer Frank Chorodov (1962), a defender of individual liberties and a critic of wars and their consequences, offers us, in an entertaining fashion, the mentality of a politician and compares it with that of the rest of the population. He divides society into honest people, dishonest people and politicians, based upon the ways in which each group thinks and on how they make their living. Setting aside the free use of some generalizations, Chorodov's ideas may serve to envision environments where the lack of political knowledge may have undesirable consequences.

Chorodov (1962) sustains that the special reputation of politicians of being corrupt is not earned. He asserts that they are not any more delinquent than other members of society that have different professions such as businessmen, farmers, doctors, lawyers, mechanics, carpenters and so on. What happens is that politicians are exposed to a closer observation by the media. It should be mentioned that Transparency International (2017) has recently published data that do not agree with Chorodov's opinion on this topic.

If we consider normal the way in which most citizens think and carry on, which is to work within the law, and twisted or devious that of those that operate out of the law, we should take as fraudulent those misrepresentations of the political mind, because they are contradictory and inconsistent. They can also be nothing more than occupational hazards (Chorodov, 1962).

Honest people, being the majority, are considered normal. They earn their living offering services or goods, within a market that establishes their value. They obey the law and adjust to it because it turns out to be the best policy. They operate *within the law*.

Delinquents, being a minority and different from the majority, are considered abnormal. They earn their living taking away others' property and doing so with the least possible danger of being apprehended. Their guiding principle is *not to get caught*. They operate *outside the law*.

Politicians may be divided into bureaucrats and elected officials. They think differently. What they have in common is that they operate *behind the law*. What differentiates the world of those that operate behind the law from the rest, is that its members exclusively work on acquiring power over citizens; these may be either normal or abnormal. They exert the monopoly of the use of coercion, inhibition and restriction. The population interprets or visualizes their actions as a specialized service. However, no specialized service of the kind offered by those that do not belong to the world behind the law enjoys the prerogative of regulating the rest of the services. On the other hand, government, with the monopoly of coercion, derived from the law, situates itself above the rest of society. Government prospers, not according to the services it renders but according to the power it has at its disposal. Unlike of what is commonly believed, government is not evaluated by its efficiency, expenditure, public debt, corruption, protection of liberties and so on, it is only judged by counting votes. The results determine if it stays or leaves. In no-voting systems, other evaluation methods are possible.

The elected official is psychologically more complex than the bureaucrat. Sometimes he thinks in a similar way as the people he represents; meaning, in a normal way. This probably happens because his power stems from the votes he receives from them; which persuades him to keep some contact. However, by carefully examining his behavior, you will find that he belongs to a different world from that of the people he represents. While these think that he is dedicated to the defense of their interests, the politician intimately knows that his interest is centered into being elected or reelected. With that in mind he takes pain into make them believe that he is a man of honor. The reality is quite different, in the words of Chorodov (1962; p. 139): *"He is out to feather his own nest, always."*

Political Representation of the Citizen

Why is it necessary for citizens to be represented in government? Because they cannot be present at all levels of government when decisions that may affect their interests are being made. If they should attempt it, no one would do any work except that. For each situation citizens authorize someone so that their rights are defended, and their preferences presented.

From the Constitution, citizens derive the most general protection. Compliance with it implies that the rest of the laws have to be upheld. The Supreme Court or equivalents are guarantors of the rule of law.

Even full compliance with the Constitution, laws, norms and regulations could be approved and upheld which do not favor interests or preferences of citizens. To prevent those types of situations, citizens elect, for fixed periods, representatives that inspire their trust. If such representatives should not honor that trust, citizens would find themselves in a weak position caused by a disloyal representation.

Within government there are posts with a great decision power, which are filled either through election or appointment. If some of these officials should take unwanted decisions, there is little that can be done to quickly correct them.

What can be done so that representatives defend the interests of citizens? In the first place it is essential that such interests be determined by taking into account expectations and desires of the whole population. This is not an easy thing to do because it entails the free expression of each citizen, the determination of ideas related to many areas and the evaluation of those that have a substantial backing. Those ideas that enjoy the stronger backings should be the ones that representatives present and defend as mandates.

Perhaps, in societies with up to several thousand citizens, it may be possible for them to express directly the interests of the collective. For practical reasons in more numerous societies such a direct and frequent communication of ideas has not been possible in the past. The collective opinion was substituted by the results of the frequent and effective communication between members of small groups of people such as courts, councils, boards, assemblies and entourages.

Representatives of the general population, because of the impracticality of the necessary exchange of ideas among citizens, do not achieve a clear collective mandate. On the other hand, this circumstance has allowed representatives to preferentially defend their own interests, those of their political parties and those of groups or individuals that may favor them.

The sad conclusion that can be derived from the above is that, in most governments, for one reason or another, there are no consistently true or loyal representatives of citizens. It should then not be surprising that, globally, the citizens' approval of governments, many of their institutions and their more visible officials should be so low. I conclude that it is essential that government structures evolve in such a way that the opinion of citizens, on all matters they may choose, may be expressed freely, directly and continually. Fortunately, as has been presented in chapter *Favorable Structures*, modern technologies allow just that: The practically instantaneous exchange of information among many millions, with the aid of the Web.

Communication among Citizens

What or who hinders such communication?
Several factors work against communication between citizens. The most frequent factors are: 1. Population dispersion; 2. Lack of an organization with capacity and coverage required; 3. The status, represented by the power structure within government; 4. Current ignorance that such communication is now possible and the lack of vision of its benefits: 5. Fear and precaution that putting it to work would serve to create inconvenient and conflictive situations; and 6. Mainly, because it has been established through time, that ideas are essentially proposed or induced *into* the population by government, political parties and the media.

Free communication between citizens and the products derived from it may introduce orientations that are contrary to customs, traditions, beliefs or laws. The products of the direct participation of the People are the building blocks that favor the establishment of citizenry as an essential source of ideas and power.

While creating and adopting the system outlined in the previous chapter, participation difficulties related to population dispersion and lack of an organization disappear, together with the ignorance of the feasibility of the system itself. The appreciation of its potential is achieved with its operation and with it, the fear of bad consequences will dispel.

The power structure of government is not used or prepared to receive or accept suggestion or ideas, and much less mandates that have the breath and the strength derived from discussions where all citizens that wish to do so participate. Legal arrangements to rectify such deficiency have to take place (see p. 139). It probably will not be an easy objective to achieve. It has to be kept in mind that, in many countries, even peaceful demonstrations and public complaints by large crowds are met within little sympathy and even with repression by their government.

Who would benefit by such communication? On one side the entire society would be served by a government that would be more responsive and more committed to the population. This would result in a greater stability than that which is achieved by political parties, since these respond to the preferences of only a fraction of the population (Pasquali, 2014b, p. 161-173). Feelings and opinions in a whole society change much slower than the changes of policies that are the result of the substitution of a political party by another.

Perhaps the most significant advantages derived from the communication between citizens and the ensued discussion of issues raised could be an increase of political knowledge in the population and the free contribution of dispersed knowledge within society. This knowledge will be freely available, at any time, to every member of such society. Its availability to government, individuals and organizations represents a great increase of human and social capital for any country.

Capital Use

Capital consists of the accumulation of goods or advantages that, at any one time, a society or a country can count upon. It may be classified according to its nature into physical or material, human, social and environmental. Each one may be either positive or negative and its worth is related to its congruous use with the rest of the capitals.

A country that has extensive marine coast lines, large rivers, mineral wealth, fertile lands, benign climates, a population with a high educational level, a citizenry that appreciates the law and obeys it, trusts the government and contributes to environmental causes, is also able to live in peace and establish agreements and collaborations with other countries would have a very high positive capital. If the same country should get involved in a civil war, its capital would become highly negative and, as a unity, it could fail.

A desirable situation for a society is one in which its four types of capitals work in conjunction and that they be positive and large. One could ask: Is there something or someone that may hinder such a conjunction? There are many. Many factors may determine the exclusion of some portion of positive capital. The following example illustrates how a material capital—groundwater—will be excluded from development of a region.

If a law exists that prohibits or penalizes the use of groundwater for agricultural use in a specific region, such activity will be reduced or made more costly and less competitive. Or, if such a law does not exist, but permission needed to drill wells for its extraction consists of a process that entails many requirements difficult to fulfill, permissions will not be requested, and no wells will be drilled. Or, if requirements to obtain the drilling permit are part of a routine, officials authorized to issue them could deny them making use of their discretionary power. Or, when the approval of permits is routine, if technical personnel to guide the localization of the drilling sites does not exists or is not available, drilling wells could turn out not to be successful or unpredictable and too risky.

Another example of a factor that hinders the proper conjunction of capitals in a country is the way in which, frequently, the parcels of power of government operate. Each department, division, direction, office etc. protects with zeal the area over which it has authority, discretion or decision power. This may result in actions internally inconsistent, costly and long-lasting. The Department of Agriculture of the Unites States of America recommends, based on scientific studies, to eat fresh fruits and vegetables as part of a diet that helps avoid a series of chronic diseases. At the same time the Department finances the Food Stamps program designed to help feeding poor families, which includes purchasing foods that it does not recommend, such as soda pops, sweets, biscuits and ice cream. The 2016 budget for the Food Stamps program was US$ 78,000 million (Edwards, 2016); a fraction of it is used to purchase products that the Department does not recommend. This is the type of inconsistency that requires attention.

It should be pointed out that these analyses can be done by anyone, because countries like the USA collect and publish the required data. Without data the common citizen cannot contribute to the efficient use of public funds.

There are many ways that may be used to hinder the efficient use of a country's capital. It is not difficult to discover them: Listen to the People. There are also many ways to invigorate the use of a country's capital: Listen to the People. However, listening to the People can be a challenge.

This is a fundamental social struggle. It implies fostering the responsibility of citizens to observe and analyze their surroundings and present ideas for improvement. It also implies the government's responsibility and willingness to make it easy for the people to express their ideas and to take them into account. Intuitively this is a substantial change. It requires the adoption of a new way of managing the relationship government-citizenry. It means the inclusion of all members of society, with their problems and expectations, knowledge, experience and capacity to innovate. This looks very much as an acceptance of a *collegial or collective power*.

Political Knowledge of the Citizen

We live in an ocean of knowledge and in an atmosphere of ignorance. Man has been able to accumulate an enormous amount of knowledge and to preserve it through very different forms of writing. The speed at which knowledge has been produced has increased through time, to the point that an individual does not have the capacity to inspect even a small fraction of it. At the same time access to information has become easier and faster.

As a result of this progress, a considerable amount of knowledge is found disseminated through the population. **The political consequence of this fact is enormous**: In order to take decisions of great general interest, it is advisable to include knowledge scattered through society. Not doing so is as senseless as going hungry surrounded by food.

Knowledge may be classified as *explicit* and *tacit*. Explicit knowledge is formal, easy to identify, file, obtain, revise, update or discard. It can be found in libraries and acquired mostly through formal education.

Tacit knowledge is personal, intuitive, based in experience; it is difficult to communicate or transfer orally or in writing, because it is tied to demonstration and direct participation. An example of this type of knowledge would be the way in which an organization assigns responsibilities to its personnel when taking decisions: It is called *know-how*.

As related to political operation it is useful to identify those social factors that can or should contribute their knowledge in different government activities. These are: 1. Government officials; 2. Common citizens; and 3. *Society*—understood as a nation or community of people with common traditions, institutions, and collective activities and interests—as indicated below.

The political knowledge of government officials, elected or appointed, should encompass, besides which is appropriate for the common citizen: 1. The Constitution and its consequences; 2. The main national or state purpose in which his office is an operating member; 3. The details of the specific job responsibilities; 4. The updated information related to matters in which he has to deal with; 5. Those institutions or people that could help with ideas, reviews, critiques and decision taking; and 6. To know how to deal with orders or arrangements that are dishonest or inconvenient.

The basic political knowledge that will allow the common citizen to express and defend his preferences in a personal or collective fashion includes: 1. The contents of the Constitution; 2. The basic public policies (public order, education, health, economy, infrastructure, administration of justice, international relations and the offices and the individuals that are responsible for each of them); 3. Structural elements of government; 4. The ideologies that may be in competition, such as democracy, conservatism, liberalism, progressivism, communism, religious fundamentalism, collectivism et cetera (Heywood, 2012); 5. The role of the citizen in society and in government: His duties, rights, and ways to defend his individual or collective interests; 6. Basic characteristics of the budget (national, state and municipal); and 7. Keeping abreast to what is going on (Somin, 2013b).

The political knowledge of the common citizen and its effect on political decisions has been studied in many countries. In general terms that knowledge is very deficient, especially when it is being compared to that of the elite made up by academics, lawyers, journalists and some others. However, with that deficient knowledge citizens take, in many cases, the same political decisions that they would have taken by having all the information needed. This fact is understood by observing that citizens, before making a decision, are guided as much as by the ideas expressed by people they consider trustworthy and knowledgeable as by the ideas expressed by people they do not trust, and act accordingly (Lupia, 2016).

Another way to analyze the political knowledge of the population is to evaluate it as related to the subject matter under consideration. When done this way, it is found that the common citizen will inform himself earnestly when the decision is about to be taken directly affects him. For example, if the approval of an international treaty to counter the effects of climate change that are estimated to take place in the next decades is under consideration, the common citizen probably would not have much to contribute and not much interest in doing so. However, if the matter under consideration is a curriculum change for his children or an increase of taxes, he will probably look for information that will serve as a basis to develop his position and will be enthused in doing so. As a consequence of this behavior, local governments are assisted and strengthened by the ideas and preferences of their citizens. Their higher efficiency and sensitivity to desires of the population make them better than distant or national governments. This fact strongly supports decentralized forms of government (Somin, 2013a).

A key characteristic of democracy and any other form of good government is its constant receptivity toward citizens' preferences. In order to be effective, citizens should be capable to express such preferences personally and collectively. If citizens do not know enough about government, it is difficult for them to demand accountability from their leaders. An evident way to increase the political knowledge of the population is through compulsory public education. In practice, this method has not produced desirable results for two reasons:

Government does not have incentives to adopt it and, when it has been done, it has been used for indoctrination (Somin, 2013b).

When a country or a society is going through a political crisis that compromises the social order, the interest of the population in political knowledge increases and creates favorable conditions for the discussion of politics. In such a case, political instruction of the population, with the aid of papers, guidebooks etc., written in simple language, may achieve acceptable levels in a short time (Pasquali, 2017). Results would be an important long-lasting advance of social capital.

Political knowledge of *society* deserves special attention. Society, as used in this section, includes, in a collegial fashion—with authority or power shared equally among colleagues—individuals and associations of individuals. It includes every citizen, academic organizations such as universities, research institutes, national academies, professional associations or societies (lawyers, medical doctors, journalists, geologists, librarians, businessmen, teachers, musicians, athletes, artists, economists, government officials et cetera), political parties, religious groups, chambers of commerce, industry chambers, non-governmental organizations (NGO) and means of public communication. Each citizen has the right to express himself/herself directly, while associations do it through their authorized spokespersons. As described, society has at its disposal the largest amount of political knowledge of a nation, be it explicit or tacit. ***As a corollary of this fact, society is a mandatory bench mark for political decisions of lasting importance***.

It is interesting to observe that political parties, whose members are generally a small fraction of the citizenry (Pasquali, 2014a; p. 153-161), have the audacity and the ability to reserve for themselves the political representation of the entire society.

The greater amount of explicit knowledge is found in archives, to many of which all humanity has access. The greater part of the knowledge of a country, that is up-to-date and available at any time, rests in the framework of society, not in government. The same could be said, even with more emphasis, about tacit knowledge. These facts should not go unnoticed.

I maintain that decisions related to essential and strategic matters, of great importance for the nation (MHGR; p. 64), must include society's knowledge, as has been described. This is especially necessary when the decision is the exclusive legal duty or responsibility of a single person. No one has enough knowledge required to take core decisions for a society, especially when attempted without consulting the wishes and preferences of its members. To leave them exclusively to government, as currently known, would mean to willfully disregard the greater portion of the human resources at its disposal. The toxic consequences of such exclusivity and their scope are illustrated by the following example.

The Institute for Strategy and Competitiveness of the Business School of Harvard University has published a study of competitiveness of the United States of America (USA) for 2016 (Porter et al., 2016). The study organizes its contents into four key areas: 1. The economy of the USA in an era of political paralysis; 2. The faltering USA economic performance; 3. An eroding USA business environment; and 4. The pressing need for a national economic strategy. For our purposes we will only consider results of *an era of political paralysis*.

The challenges of the present economy of the USA require the understanding of what competitiveness is and what prosperity implies. These terms are described in the following quote (Porter et al., 2016): *"A nation is competitive if it creates the conditions where two things occur simultaneously: businesses operating in the nation can (1) compete successfully in domestic and international markets, while (2) maintaining and improving the wages and living standards of the average citizen. When these occur together, a nation prospers. When one occurs without the other, a nation is not truly competitive, and prosperity is not sustainable. If business succeeds but the average worker is losing ground, or when worker incomes rise but businesses can no longer compete, the nation is not competitive. A hallmark of a competitive economy, then, is prosperity that is widely shared. And without successful businesses, there can be no jobs and no long-run income growth."*

Competitiveness of the USA has been decreasing since before the Great Depression of the past century. Its causes are not cyclic but structural and associated to a lack of capacity to deal with them. A stumbling political system of the USA leads to stabilization of a lack of progress of government performance, especially in what relates to federal government. Porter et al. (2016) state that the current political system of the USA is the greater obstacle to economic progress of the nation. Another report on the same subject by Klitgaard and Light (2005), published eleven years before, reached similar conclusions. Since no changes were introduced in those eleven years, it means that the system has suffered from a lack of capacity to adapt to new circumstances. Both, the leaders of the business sector and the general public, think that government is hindering economic growth and competitiveness of the country.

Causes that prevent progress and determine the poor performance of the USA political system are multiple and complex (Porter et al., 2016). Their indications are: The decrease in activities of the Legislative Power (Congress), the loss of citizens' trust in their legislators, the poor approval level of the Executive Power, which reached its lowest rating in 2015 (when only one in five people trusted that government was doing the right thing), and the increased polarization fostered by the dominant parties. The competing presidential candidates—year 2016—have increased and deepened negative feelings in their followers, while a fraction of the population has left its political party and became independent.

The basis for the lack of trust observed is that problems have not been solved. Government seems to be paying attention to what is happening within political parties and has neglected the people. While the common citizen is not achieving positive results, political parties and other elements of the political system are being favored.

Political reforms have been frequently proposed for the electoral system, the control of the Legislative Power by political parties, lobbying and the limit to the time members of Congress may remain in office.

It may be concluded that the root of toxicity of the USA political system is the fact that political parties have been able to establish their dominance over the government structures and prevent any change that does not suit them, even if these changes should be necessary for the country's progress. The knowledge is there but it is not put to good use.

The chosen example has been analyzed, not only to understand competitiveness and prosperity of the USA but also to visualize if the same causes have an influence on the government's disapproval by citizens on the global scale (see Table 4, p. 35). The USA is a great country. It has a government that, although it requires improvements, has worked sufficiently well for the country to be recognized as a world power, with an economy that is better than those of many other countries, that has supported the highest military budget and a first-class scientific research effort, and has achieved a per capita Gross Domestic Product that has served to attract foreigners who wish to be part of its population.

The government of the USA has a structure that is similar to that of many other countries. Is it probable that those other countries could have prevented their political parties, instead of working mainly for themselves, give first priority to taking care of the interest of their citizenry and their nation? I believe it not likely. The main objective of political parties is to gain power and keep it; other objectives could get in their way.

Political parties have accomplished an important function in the historical evolution of governments. They have been essential in the evolution of monarchies, empires, fiefs and tyrannies et cetera, towards social orders with more citizens' participation and more compliance to human rights; such as republics and democracies. As political parties, through time, increased their power with respect to other components of government, such as councils and courts, they have ceased to be effective ways of citizen participation in government matters and have turned into monopolies that compete among themselves in the pursuit of power. This transformation has created a toxicity that requires an antidote.

For the good of the future of societies of *Homo sapiens*, the current government structures have to evolve towards more intense and better-quality citizen participation and representation. Political parties should not be allowed to control government or society. In order to achieve such a state of affairs, government has to follow suggestions and mandates that come from discussion between all citizens that wish to participate. This can be obtained with the use of modern communication techniques and collective intelligence.

Political parties are not the only factors that work against citizens' participation and representation. The most important factor is the lack of communication between citizens. Others are: Monarchies, dictatorships, tyrants, governments with only one political party, pretensions of the military, biased media, religious fundamentalism, some ideologies, tribal systems, some electoral systems, long periods of representatives in their posts, decisions taken by few individuals and a deficient political formation of the population.

Under these conditions, no one should be surprised that worldwide approval of governments is low, that they do not operate as well as they could, and that economic and social progress of societies and nations is challenging.

The most important governmental political acts are decisions and their monitoring, because they are the courses of action that determine the future. A rational decision represents a compromise between unlike objectives (Adam, 2012; Pomerol and Adam, 2004). Decision taking is a process that implies conditioning information and a development in phases. The process consists of: 1. Identification of all possible alternatives; 2. Determination of all possible consequences of those alternatives; and 3. Evaluation of all identified consequences.

From the observation of discussions that have taken place in some political bodies, such as assemblies and congresses, I got the impression that they take decisions in a disorderly manner, frequently substituting oratory for information, subordinate interests for possible alternatives and oblivion for probable consequences. It certainly is not a recommended way to reach decisions on public matters.

Decisions taken by the Executive Power are more difficult to analyze because they develop out of the public domain, generally by one person or a few. They may affect from the operation of a small department up to the destiny of a nation. It has been already mentioned that, when matters on which decisions have to be taken have important and long-lasting consequences, it is not wise that they be dealt by one person or a small group; all those that have enough knowledge to analyze, criticize or offer alternatives should, on time, take part in it. The following quote from Thomas Sowell gives support to the idea: *"It is hard to imagine a more stupid or more dangerous way of making decisions than by putting those decisions in the hands of people who pay no price for being wrong."*

Fortunately, a good communication between citizens, methodical, orderly and constant may be the right antidote that has the power to correct, not only a deficient representation but also most toxicities that human societies have to endure. An effective way to achieve it is to insert into government an additional independent power whose core mission will be to organize, support, maintain and make use of the results of such communication.

The next chapter *Inclusive Power* will explore this new structure.

INCLUSIVE POWER

"Educate the whole mass of the people ... They are the only sure reliance for the preservation of our liberty."

"Leave no authority existing not responsible to the people."
Thomas Jefferson

"You never change things by fighting the existing reality. To change something, build a new model that makes the existing model obsolete."
R. Buckminster Fuller

Introduction

The central purpose of this work is the search for the improvement of conditions at which the individual is exposed within his society. In theory, the Constitution, the Declaration of Human Rights and the voting power during elections, confer a great importance to those conditions. On the other hand, indices and data related to different aspects of life in world's societies, show that there is an extensive disagreement of citizens with the performance of their government. This situation sets a difficult stage for the improvement, regulation and management of the relationship citizen-society. While the law seems to protect citizens, a very significant fraction of them doesn't conform to the results obtained by the current arrangement.

The individual is the weakest part of society and requires protection of his natural rights: To choose, according to his natural abilities, a way to earn a living, to acquire an education similar to that of the rest of citizens, and to thrive. Additionally, he should have the right and the means to directly defend himself. His main legal duties are to have a socially acceptable behavior and to contribute financially to the operation of government.

The individual requires protection due to the fact that an organization is more powerful than any one individual. Because of it, society or government may impose upon him either by direct force or the fear of it. An expression that illustrates this fact, which I take from a friend that I met during field work, summarizes it: *"Two will bind a third one."* (see Figure 1, p. 4). It serves to point out that an individual may be overpowered or lose his liberty if two others organize themselves and decide to subjugate him. Please notice that my friend did not say: *"Between five will bind four others"*; in this case the situation would be more complex, because it would pit two organizations of similar power, in which other factors come into play in order to foretell probable outcomes.

The *two* of the quote make up the simplest social organization that I know. Its simplicity should not lead to the underestimation of the effects that may be derived from it. What would happen if those *two that bind a third* decide to go on indefinitely with their original action? Well, they would overpower all of us, one by one.

Although my old friend's expression only illustrates the case in which physical and bodily strength is used, the same domination process can be extended with the use of laws, regulations, norms, arms, procedures, traditions, customs, instructions, delays, discretions et cetera. They are the tools used by politicians that operate *behind the law* to coerce, as described by Chorodov (1962; see p. 81). Government has many tools that can be used to pressure citizens and control their will or conduct.

The power of government is such that, not only can it pressure citizens but can also strongly pressure organizations in its areas of influence. Government structures, laws and power are essential to the fulfillment of its responsibilities: However, there are structures, laws and procedures that are not needed, and there are others that are clearly toxic. They have been adopted or created under conditions that were different from the current ones or without taking into account preferences, problems and alternatives for the wellbeing of the population. Frequently they have been approved or instituted by a government that has concentrated too much power but has lost the capacity to correct or adjust itself to new conditions. It is a government that causes damage to its society and is losing prestige and stability. It has reached a regressive stage; its future and that of society are not promising. The devise and rehearse of solutions that offer possibilities for reverting course, avert crises and sufferings of the population are in order.

Several lines of evidence concur in that the main causes of social instability, lack of adaptability to new conditions and inacceptable use of the available human, social and material capital are consequences of common government structures.

The existing basic structure of Executive—Legislative—Judiciary Powers operates essentially without efficient control, supervision, or adjustment dictated by the population it governs. This model, based on the concentration of power, which is supported by its electoral system, is obsolete and in need of substitution by a model which incorporates direct representation.

The electoral process in general use, whose intent is supposed to give citizens the power to select the magistrates for the main government posts, does precisely the opposite, it strips from citizens their basic political power to represent themselves.

As a first illustration of this statement, let us examine an election for a representative of an electoral circuit to Congress or Parliament by the voters of that circuit. The ballot overwhelmingly shows candidates postulated by political parties, because the organization and funding of campaigns are not to be found in the non-partisan population. This means that the independent voter—which in most cases constitutes a majority—if he/she chooses to vote, must vote for a candidate that belongs to a political party and, as a consequence, will feel obligation and loyalty toward that political party.

The most interesting consequence of the victory of a candidate is that he/she will represent in Congress or Parliament all the people of his/her electoral district; which includes those that voted for him/her and also those that did not. This means that, as far as defending or representing the interests, likings and preferences of the people, he/she cannot have a clear idea of what he/she should defend. Of course, that would be in addition to the loyalty that is due to the partisans that got him/her on the ballot. The conclusion to be derived is that, elections as they are generally set up cannot result in a loyal or true representation of the people.

The saddest part of this arrangement is that citizens have, willingly and happily, or not, participated in a process by which their political power of representing themselves has been transferred to someone else, who will use it legally at his/her discretion. After casting a vote, for or against the winner, voters are politically dead; they may as well go into a political coma or a political vegetative state until the next election, when they will regain consciousness for enough time to cast their vote and, by doing so, start another cycle of political auto-nullification.

What does this do to government? At least five things: 1. It becomes insensitive to the society it is supposed to serve; 2. It drifts into a stagnant state dominated by political parties and bureaucracy; 3. It operates without effective direction and supervision by the people; 4. It loses its ability to adjust to changing political conditions; and 5. It will not be able to make good use of much of the human, social and material capital of the nation.

Can this electoral process be fixed, or should it be discarded? It can be fixed. It should not be discarded because all citizens cannot be present through the process of drafting laws; the number or persons needed for the job is small and, for reasons of cost, has an upper limit. However, members of Congress or Parliament should be elected as *agents*, not *representatives*. This means that citizens retain their political power. Laws are drafted and presented, and citizens decide if they should be enacted or not. This added step, an expression of collective power, would cost nothing, if a system such as has been presented as part of the Inclusive Power is adopted; it will be just another discussion item that requires a decision (see p. 64 and p. 145).

In some countries the text of a new law is sent to the President for acceptance and signing, and to the Judiciary for a constitutionality check. There, the text may be objected, either because its content is not acceptable and sent back for a change or because of unconstitutionality and sent back for adaptation to the Constitution. This procedure may be used as an example of the advantages of the *balance of power* in a democratic government, acting in favor of the wellbeing of the people. It can also be considered as an example of *the complete exclusion of the direct political power of the people* in important government matters. If differences between the Executive, Legislative and Judiciary Powers arise, I believe it will be welcomed news, because it brings to public light an important issue that should be resolved. I do not think correct or constructive or desirable that such an issue should be resolved with the victory or the defeat of powers that have equivalent standings; that is, they are *derived* from the delegation of the *direct* power of citizens. I think that such an issue should be discussed and resolved by making use of the collective intelligence of society embodied in the Inclusive Power.

A second illustration of consequences associated with the present electoral process is the election of the President of a democratic government or a similar post. A common practice is that political parties and other organizations propose their candidates to the electorate. There will be a campaign where each candidate will present a set of issues and a program that he/she will follow to solve them. There will be a lot of promises, good intentions and disposition, praise to himself/herself, denigration of other candidates, pictures, speeches, contributions of funds and people looking for future appointments. Generally, there will not be much written material about the candidates' curricula vitae or data that could be used as indicators of honesty, compassion, integrity, flexibility, judgment and responsibility, which are some qualities that are mentioned as highly desirable for statesmanship.

When a winner emerges and takes power is when difficulties appear. The main problem that I perceive is that the President does not clearly know *what* should be done. Some actions are very obvious and urgent: The appointment of ministers of the Executive, a group of advisers, consultants and assistants. These will turn out to be important in the determination of what actually will be done or attempted. One of their effects will be to shield the President from the rest of the nation. The President will become impervious to the direct opinion and contribution of society. Unpleasant opinions will mostly come from self-serving political adversaries that are preparing a candidate with which to substitute him/her in the following presidential election.

The President will also inherit a multitude of programs and projects that are within the dominion of the established bureaucracy and that take care of most of the available budget. The President will have to deal with the complexities of the Legislative

Power in order to get approval of funds for what he/she promised during the campaign.

What I am painting is a situation of a President, extremely busy with ceremonial, political, economic and cultural activities that will not allow his/her dedication to those responsibilities that the Constitution assigns to the post. In order to do a good job, he/she will have to choose, from all actions that are viable, *those that are most wanted by the People.*

Under present circumstances society does not have the ways or the means to discuss collectively what People want and expect from government. The system described as the main tool for the operation of the Inclusive Power, allows society to discuss and decide collectively such wanted actions.

With a clear mandate from the People the President does not have to study or develop political philosophy to decide what is best for his society. He/she can immediately act as an Executive and concentrate on achieving expected results. The People will recognize his/her performance; he/she will also stand out among Presidents.

The new government model, based on direct representation of the People, will retain the traditional Executive, Legislative and Judiciary Powers, and add the Inclusive Power (IP). IP will function as an association of citizens engaged in a common pursuit, will operate with collegiality, where authority and power is shared equally among colleagues; a very powerful feature for the unity of the college. The function of IP is to provide government with direction, supervision, control and adjustment to new conditions, based on *society's collective knowledge*. The direction is provided by the determination of missions of high government responsibility (MHGRs; p. 64). Supervision is provided through citizen's observations, which will lead to analysis, discussion and advisement. Control is provided through discussion of new actions or policies of government that need approval of IP, such as new laws to be enacted. Adjustment to new conditions is provided through the analysis of government organizations, policies, laws, taxes, treaties, agreements et cetera, that may seem outdated or that should be created; they will be discussed, and conclusions sent to the appropriate office.

Another function of IP is to accept for discussion, from any citizen, topics which have some relationship with social matters. Such discussions will also produce information with potential business applications, such as marketing. Who would not like to know what citizens wish to discuss? There should be a lot of interest in giants such as Google, Facebook, Amazon, Baidu, Yahoo and the like. Such information will certainly be useful for marketing and, especially, for the selection of investment projects; hence for the progress of the nation.

I have criticized current electoral systems and their unfortunate consequences, but I have not suggested replacements. I found it to be a complex problem whose solution belongs to each society, preferably by making use of its collective intelligence. Chronologically, the adoption of IP will come first and with it the installment of its system for discussion. Such system can be used to develop new electoral procedures during the transition period from the old to the new government model. I would expect that these new procedures will follow the same principles used for national elections, as for the state-county-region and municipal governments.

Analysis of data and indices of approval of governments at the global level led me to conclude that they can frequently be oppressive and subjugating organizations. The commonly-cited *balance of powers* in democracies, advertised as an important factor for their quality and stability, just does not exist. Much to the contrary, we may refer to it as a noxious imbalance of power, since the collective power of the People, even if at all recognized, is compromised, neutralized or reduced.

The media, which in theory should mediate between society and politics, frequently, are not able to do a respectable job. At times, media tries to maintain autonomy and hegemony and, at other times, integrates with government policies. In general, news in the media are filtered to regulate the content of public information and communication to the political system (Moniruzzaman, 2018; and references therein).

The balance of power that is essential for the stability and quality of government and society is that which is capable of defining and limiting government's responsibilities and of controlling its performance. It is achievable with the empowerment of *society's collective knowledge.*

Power is exercised through decisions. These may be arrived at in different ways. Currently most decisions are taken by elites that usually, but not always, are prepared and adroit solving problems. Decisions derived from the collective knowledge of citizens could or should be taken by a large number of people. This procedure implies the input of a large number of experiences, points of view, data, purposes and aspirations.

For the good of society, it is important to know if superior ways to reach good decisions exist. Of special interest would be to know the results of comparing decisions' quality between those taken by elites versus those taken by a large number of citizens.

This comparison of methods has been done for the solution of problems in different areas. For several of these areas it has been established that, in general, the contribution of a large number of people, that have a high degree of knowledge diversity, produces better decisions than those achieved by a few well-informed, experienced and intelligent people (Hong and Page, 2004).

In the field of politics Landemore (2014a; 2014b; and references therein), has asserted and defended that democracy—inclusive and egalitarian, where all participate, and all have the same rights—may be considered as an effective collective way to search for solutions to social problems. It has been called a heuristic method since it may use experimental and trial-and-error methods.

During the analysis of political problems, it is frequent that doubts related to a specific problem include the very nature of solutions being sought, their number and the probabilities of them being successful (Landemore, 2014a). Landemore's research led her to conclude that *the inclusion of all is a suitable rational index for diversity of knowledge.* This index is a weighty factor in solving problems that require an ample distribution of perspectives, talents and preferences. On the other hand, as a consequence of the type of uncertainties that are inherent to politics, equality of political rights for all is found to be essential for the achievement of the best solutions. Briefly stated, the conclusion reached is that, as a first approximation, when collectively dealing with the unknown, the participation of all—where none has different rights from the rest—it is still the simplest, quickest and more intelligent way to reach the best political decisions.

This conclusion finds invaluable evidence from the Golden Age of Athenian culture, which took place from 508 to 322 B.C. During this period of 186 years Athens had only two oligarchic governments, one in years 411 to 410 B.C. and the other in years 404 to 403 B.C.; both were imposed externally and each one did not last more than a few months. The rest of the Golden Age was one of ample democratic participation that involved regular and successful decisions taken by large groups of people. Such a stable arrangement enjoyed general support, was preserved with zeal and adopted by other city-states (Moore, 1983; Weiner, 2016).

The system outlined in chapter *Favorable Structures* contains the essential characteristics for the adoption of the direct participation of citizens in government matters through the new independent power called here **Inclusive Power**. This power acquires a legitimate origin by formalizing the effective participation of each citizen, according to the human rights of free expression and association and allowing the addition of the human capital of the whole nation. With the rank of *independent power,* it will also achieve recognition from the other powers.

The introduction of this new power will be accompanied by a change in the conception of government, in the ways in which government receives guidelines for its operation and in the ways it will be held accountable for results achieved.

Currently government—Executive, Legislative and Judicial Powers—without encumbrances, select and change their functions and their responsibilities within those that are stated in the Constitution; determines policies, prepares budgets, approves them, and adjusts taxes to cover expenses. If the adjustment should turn out to be inconvenient or insufficient, it will go into debt during the present administration or for as long as needed. The government is the Boss, the opinions and feelings of the common citizens have a very weak influence on what the government is going to do.

To be precise and just we should recognize that Government has a structure and a set of laws that limit or indicate that such is the legal way for it to operate. On the other hand, *Government does not receive from society a clear and specific mandate of what is expected by the People.* It seems very clear and supported by evidence that, under the present circumstances, what will be done is what the present rulers think appropriate or what is convenient to them. And it is perfectly legal.

By the time the new **Inclusive Power** has been adopted and is part of government, I envision a government that has received a clear mandate from society, which includes the selected areas of high government responsibility (MHGRs) and no others. With this mandate, just as has been presented in chapter *Favorable Structures* (p. 56), the structural changes required for the adjustment to the new vision of government will commence. This phase should not take more than a couple of years. In each country, states, cities and municipalities will also have their own priority areas. The time for this reorganization will depend on the current structure and the MHGRs that have been decided.

From the beginning of this major adjustment period onward, government will rely on the direction and support of the People. It is important to have full awareness and appreciation of what this signifies. Expected effects include: 1. Offices, plans and projects that have similar functions or goals within the same MHGR will be combined and, if they are not related to any MHGR, they will be eliminated; 2. The Inclusive Power, constantly analyzes, discusses and reaches conclusions on ways to better government performance, and offers them to those organizations that can make use of them; 3. Political polarization caused by political parties disappears, because ideas are not treated as proposals put forward by political parties or other organizations: They are initiated and discussed by citizens as individuals; 4. It will not be necessary or useful for the population to organize public demonstrations in order to present complaints, because they may be initiated, presented to public consideration, and transformed into conclusions. These will be sent to responsible agencies with recommendations or mandates of the Inclusive Power; 5. Evidence of incompetence, negligence, corruption or fault related to government agencies or officials may be submitted to the Inclusive Power at any time by any citizen. It will be analyzed, substantiated or discarded, and action taken as decided; and 6. Feelings of not belonging, resignation, desolation and being of no consequence in their own country, that citizens may have, will disappear, since an easy way to directly contribute to public matters exists. Those feelings will be substituted by comfort and pride for having a voice that will be heard.

Diagnosis

Over time monarchs, emperors, dictators, theocrats, legislators and, especially, political parties have built legal frameworks that hinder the introduction of changes and controls required to preserve individual liberties and to promote social progress (Gates, 2005; Atlee, 2012). The resulting inflexibility comes with decreasing economic and government effectiveness and accompanied by deterioration of quality of life of the population. Frequently, to make things worse, a vicious circle is established by a sickly government tendency to add responsibilities and budget needs. This process, *which goes on without control of those that pay the bills*, increases the range and the magnitude of social problems.

Confronted by this situation, political parties do very little else besides taking turns to govern. The operator which commands the same obsolete machinery is what is being changed: No meaningful improvement, just wasting time.

A similar process—one that also goes on without the control of those that pay the bills—occurs when nations unite through a government that is one level further from the citizen, such as what happens with the European Union. The present time shows the failure of this type of arrangement with, for example, the adoption of general migration and economy policies that go against the will of the populations of member countries.

The legal framework described does not only hinder government's change, it also distances people from government. When citizens decide to demonstrate collectively a complaint directed to government, which was previously presented by other means; instead of being received with the disposition to discuss or deal with the complaint, are frequently received as enemies of the public order and repressed by the police, as the laws and procedures indicate, and as discretion allows.

When this happens, it is because the government has lost its compass, it shows its inability to honor the service that has already been paid for and whose quality is being challenged. The client and at the same time co-owner or shareholder is being mistreated or oppressed.

Law and order is essential for every society, and so are the organizations that uphold them by force. They have to help protect life and properties of the population by means determined by existing norms. A common serious problem is that the *order* that has been established has been shaped without the suggestions, preferences or knowledge of citizens, without their approval and without the precaution of an effective oversight. I am convinced that an effective oversight of government can only be achieved by the power of the People. *The most powerful force in a democracy should reside in its citizenry, well informed and active.* This means that a government that is managed only by agents and representatives is not capable of maintaining a performance that reflects the desires of the governed. Such a government is incomplete. Until the governed, in a collective fashion, are not in control of government, it will not keep a stable course. The adoption of an Inclusive Power corrects this situation.

A similar posture is illustrated in the quote of Ludwig von Mises: *"Corruption is an inherent fault of every Government that is not under the control by public opinion."* Another, belonging to Luis E. Alcalá, while discussing the adoption of a new political course for the Venezuelan government, addressed the People and said (2017a): *"To command is to be preferred to protest and to demand."* Alcalá indicated that the People should speak with the authority of the Crown.

The position supported here adds to the above the way to obtain the opinion of the People. Von Mises, as stated by the quote, could admit or suggest that such opinion or view is expressed by the media; a statement that I do not share (see pp. 113-114). Here I put forward and defend that the authorized public opinion has to be the result of the exchange of ideas and the evaluation of alternatives where each citizen has the same rights as any other. I hasten to note that one quote should not be taken as a summary of a person's thoughts on a subject; von Mises may have expressed, depending on context, different ideas on the same subject.

Alcalá's expression is very close to the position adopted here, especially when he adds that: *"Above all, the People have to participate, it is the People who have to compare proposals and, perhaps, they may be their own doctor."*

Recently I became aware of a proposal presented by Luis Enrique Alcalá in 1994, and restated (Alcalá, 2017b) as the Republic's Yearly Referendum (*Referendo Anual de la República*, in Spanish). This Referendum is directed to the approval or disapproval of the President (of the country), based on his performance during his latest year in office. It would take place after he has presented his annual report and before the date he would be confirmed or not confirmed for the following year. The Referendum has been devised as a formal control of the Sovereign Power of the People, to be established in the Constitution through an amendment.

Alcalá's proposal goes in the same direction as the Inclusive Power presented in this book; which is the empowerment of the People to control Government

(Alcalá, 2017b). It seems significant that, Alcalá and I, separately, would reach a common Constitutional answer to the problem caused by the current lack of strength and frequency of formal and legal input of the population into governmental matters.

Inclusive Power differs from the Republic's Yearly Referendum, in that the control of the People is based on discussions and decisions that take place continuously and in a way that allows corrections, suggestions and ideas to be expressed at any time they are reached. Such decisions will not deal only with the Executive Power but extend to all powers established in the Constitution.

Function of the Inclusive Power

The essential mission of the Inclusive Power is to continuously express what the citizenry expects from its government. This is achieved through an effective communication, where all citizens may participate thanks to the use of the Web. Additional communication methods may be added in situations where the Web does not reach or work.

What the citizenry expects from its government requires some precision. There are many areas that have to be considered by citizens and, all those that desire to be involved, will have the opportunity to do so. These basic conditions will ensure that a great amount of information will be exchanged, and many discussions will take place. Much time and work will be involved in ordering ideas, deliberate, select alternatives and, finally, determine which have enough support to be considered as representative.

At the start of activities of the Inclusive Power the most urgent task is to determine those missions that will become the main responsibility of government (MHGR), and to what extent or degree. The MHGRs selected are used to define the government structure. At the same time, they will help determine the degree of taxation required to fund an efficient operation.

Benefits that result from a reorganization based on the defined MARGs will be illustrated with an example, using data of the Executive Power of the Venezuelan government for December of 2016.

Although this case is not very common or typical, was chosen because its structure gives no clear indication of which are the greater goals of the nation (see pp. 65-68). It may be contrasted with other structures that allow those goals to be clearly envisaged.

Of this Executive Power, because of its complexity and extent, only those components that are related to the distribution of functions and responsibilities will be mentioned. It includes the Presidency, Vice-Presidency and Ministries. The names of the ministries include the expression *Ministry of the Popular Power for* (MMPM) and their list follows:

1. MMMP Revolutionary Transformation of the Great Caracas.
2. MMMP Prison System.
3. MMMP University Education, Science and Technology.
4. MMMP Water and Air Transportation.
5. MMMP Industries.
6. MMMP Health.
7. MMMP Social Work Process.
8. MMMP Defense.
9. MMMP Internal Relations, Justice and Peace.
10. MMMP Ecosocialism and Waters.
11. MMMP Nutrition.
12. MMMP Culture.
13. MMMP Tourism.
14. MMMP Youth and Sports.
15. MMMP Communication and Information.
16. MMMP Women and Gender Equality.
17. MMMP Communes and Social Movements.
18. MMMP Agriculture and Lands.
19. MMMP the Economy, Finance and Public Banking.
20. MMMP Foreign Relations.
21. MMMP Housing, Habitat and Ecosocialism.
22. MMMP Oil and Mining.
23. MMMP Electric Energy.
24. MMMP of the Office of the Presidency, and Follow-up of the Government Management.
25. MMMP Native People.
26. MMMP Education.
27. MMMP Ground Transportation.
28. MMMP Planning and Finance.
29. MMMP Commerce.
30. MMMP Fisheries and Agriculture.
31. MMMP Urban Agriculture.

It should be noted that, besides the ministries listed, the MMMP of the Office of the Presidency, and Follow-up of the Government Management includes the Vice-Presidency. This office coordinates or manages a group of formal organizations and a series of programs, both of national rank. This group is composed by: 1. National Superintendence of Internal Audit; 2. State Aeronautics Service; 3. Bolivarian National Intelligence Service; and 4. National Human Rights Council.

The series of programs contain organizations that may operate as executive offices, institutes, foundations or companies; they are called Missions (M) or Great Missions (GM). They are of very different sizes as far as the number of officials and the people they serve; they span from a few dozen to hundreds of thousands; may be attached to different entities of the Executive Power for their management or funding. They are created by presidential decrees. They add up to close to forty. For illustration purposes, the names of some of them follow: M Asphalt Party, GM Agro Venezuela, GM To All Life Venezuela, GM Greater Love, GM Sons and Daughters of Venezuela, GM Knowledge and Work, GM Housing Venezuela, M Alma Mater, M Neighborhood Sports, M New Neighborhood, M Tricolor Neighborhood, M Efficiency or Nothing, M Venezuela Electric, M Young People of the Country, M Neighborhood Mothers "Josefa Joaquina Sánchez", M Transportation, M April 13th, M Nutrition, M Tree, M Deep into Neighborhood, M Che Guevara, M Science, M Christ, M Culture, M Guaicaipuro (an old Indian chief), M Identity, M Miracle, M Miranda, M Music, M Child Jesus M Girls and Boys of the Neighborhood, M Piar, M Energetic Revolution, M Ribas, M Robinson I, M Robinson II, M Smile, M Sucre and M Zamora. The areas of influence of each one was posted on the Web link: www.gobiernoenlínea.gob.ve/misiones.dot.

In chapter *Favorable Structures* eight missions of the highest responsibility for any government (MHGR) were selected. For the government of the USA, Gates (2005) has suggested eleven as a desirable number. The Executive Power of Venezuela had, at least, three times more ministries than the recommended number of MARGs. This means, either Venezuela has not structured its government according to its MHGRs or there was not a clear idea of them. Venezuela experienced coordination difficulties when the participations of two or more ministries were required for a common program.

The evidence for these difficulties is found in the frequent restructuring undergone by ministries. For example, one of them is related to the Ministry of Public Works, which was founded in 1824. In 1977 it was divided into three ministries (Environment and Natural Renewable Resources, Urban Development, and Transportation and Communication); in 1999 the Ministry of Infrastructure was created by fusion of the Ministry of Urban Development with the Ministry of Transportation and Communications; in 2009 the Ministry of Public Works and Housing was created and the Ministry of Housing and Habitat, and Ministry of Infrastructure were eliminated; finally, in 2010 the Ministry of Transportation and Communications was created and the Ministry of

Public Works and Housing was eliminated. This Executive Power did not have great difficulties undertaking structural changes!

Its characteristics evidence that: 1. Government had difficulties associating and distributing activities or functions between several ministries; 2. Government was not satisfied with results of the many and different structures it created; 3. While organizations were being created and eliminated, their performances diminished due to the corresponding transition periods, which are frequently disruptive. This is probably the reason for the introduction of multiple organizations—the so-called Missions—each with a specific goal and outside the traditional Ministry structure; 4. The introduction of some Missions had some highly negative consequences. Among them is the assignment of additional social and financial responsibilities to the state oil company Petróleos de Venezuela (PDVSA) that were unrelated to its core purpose—which is the development of the oil and gas industry. The new responsibilities assigned to PDVSA caused a decline in its productivity, technical capacity and investment power; and 5. Government demonstrated a disposition to undertake structural changes. This disposition, in the future, perhaps, will allow it to remedy an inconvenient structure.

If a structure based on the eight MHGRs proposed (pp. 64-65) would be adopted, it would be easy to decide to which new ministry all activities coming from the old thirty-one Ministries and those of each of the Missions should be assigned. A structure where each ministry has the responsibility of managing one of the MHGRs would be established. The structure of each ministry would include all those agencies that are essential for the achievement of its central purpose. These agencies would be coordinated by the exclusive authority of the Minister. The responsibility for the achievement of goals would fall only on the Minister, who would be evaluated on that basis. There could not be excuses or reasons for failures attributable to the lack of coordination between agencies.

It would be useful to be able to predict or estimate or measure performance differences between a government whose structure has been inherited from historical conditions and one with a structure derived from MHGRs defined by the citizenry (or by other methods). Unfortunately, there are no available data to make such a quantitative comparison. I made a rough estimation of what it would mean for Venezuela to change from its December of 2016 structure to a structure based on the eight MHGRs mentioned in pages 64 and 65. I found that such change would decrease the government budget and the number of employees to half of what it was in 2016. This estimation finds support on the fact that, between 1999 and 2014, the number of public servants doubled.

In 2014, for every 100 employees in the private sector of the formal economy, there were 49 government employees in its formal structure; equivalent to a 33 per cent of the formal labor force (Infobae, 2015). The government with the new structure has only half the employees and is of a similar size as the 1999 government and employs 17 per cent of the country's labor force. This change would be an enormous organizational achievement since it results in a substantial decrease in public spending, while maintaining the same government services. By transferring half of its employees to private production areas it would create a period of rapid economic growth. The change would foster a more efficient way to use society's human capital directed toward goals selected by the People.

To ensure that such will be the case, the People, through the Inclusive Power, will have the opportunity to give their opinions, contribute to their discussion, and determine those MHGRs that are needed. There should be no fear that the "ignorant mob" would reach decisions that make no sense, as sometimes it is speculated or alerted (Atlee, 2012). Society, as it has been previously described, possesses the major portion of the country's knowledge—ready to be used. On any one subject chosen for discussion, at the beginning, when opinions are presented, there will be a great variety of them. As discussion develops with the aid of key information, knowledge will be concentrated by the system and dispersed through the population.

For each specific topic anonymous leaders will emerge, because of their knowledge or their ability to interpret the available information and visualize alternatives. These alternatives, in turn, will be reduced to a few possible solutions, that will be tested for citizens' support; which would no longer be considered an "ignorant mob", but would now be a conscious crowd. This is the characteristic process employed by *collective intelligence*, which usually produces better results than individual intelligence (Helbing, 2017).

For those that may doubt that this procedure is feasible and that it can lead to good results will be glad to learn that a similar process took place in Iceland, where a group of 1,500 citizens, randomly selected, with some help for the legal expression, and the simultaneous contribution of the whole population, prepared the text of a new Constitution for their country. This experience has been published. It starts with the following text: *"Never again can the world be told by the custodians of the old that the people cannot be relied upon to write the contract between citizens and government, and write it well"* (Bater, 2011). The reading of the whole article is recommended.

Given its considerable potential for obtaining solutions to problems in different areas, collective intelligence has been the object of research in recent years. It is thought that it underlies or is responsible for the extraordinary success of *Homo sapiens*. One of the key components of collective intelligence is the formation of precise and shared beliefs. This result emerges with the use of information that is discussed among individuals wherefrom arises shared rationality (Krafft et al., 2016).

Google has invested several years to find out what characteristics distinguish very productive discussion groups from others. Project Aristotle, dedicated to such research, found that in each group, unwritten patterns and rules develop and determine the group's operation. Success of each group depends on how the members of the group relate to each other. In groups of high productivity members speak approximately the same amount of time, have a high average of social sensitivity (are conscious of how the rest of the members think and feel), perceive that they may take risks without paying for negative consequences, and there exist mutual trust and respect that allow them act naturally, without pretending. Other conditions are: Having a clear mind and group culture. The five requisites to Google's working group success have been summarized as follows: Psychological security, reliability, structure, clarity, and significance and impact of their work.

These requisites are applicable to any group, either with few or many individuals that use discussion as a method for problem solving. Groups such as Senate, Congress and Assembly of legislative powers of governments, are typically hardly able to comply with several of these requisites; which may explain their poor performance and low approval that they frequently get from the population.

The results of real-life political discussions summoned to solve social problems, have been compared with the results obtained by methods that do not require coordination between citizens, such as the selection of alternatives by votes. Studies indicate that over 30 per cent of all discussions produce no results, which gives support to the expression: *"If you wish for no action, appoint a commission to take care of the matter."* At the same time, discussions that produce good results are characterized by a flow of ideas, a balanced intervention of participants and by the way they expressed themselves. Surprisingly, it has been sustained that the analysis of the language used in the first 20 seconds of the meeting allows for the prediction of the result of the discussion (Niculae, 2016). If these results should be applicable to the collegiate bodies of legislative powers, as they probably are, it would be wise to be thinking of an evolution of those powers.

Application of collective intelligence to the solution of social problems has been tested by governments of several countries; among them the Unites States of America, Canada, South Korea, Australia and Ireland. During 2011 OGP (Open Government Partnership) was created. It consists of a multilateral government initiative whose goal is to reach concrete commitments for promoting transparency, *sharing power with the citizenry*, fighting corruption and using new technologies to improve governance, in an ambient of cooperation between allies. To be members of this alliance governments have to sign the Declaration of Open Government, submit an action plan that has been consulted with the citizenry and commit to inform on the progress of such action plan (OGP, 2011). The Alliance in its Declaration includes the majority of those matters that should include civic society's opinion.

For the purpose of this chapter two aspects of the operation of Alliance OGP will be mentioned: 1. Unwillingness of government to share information and sustain a dialog with citizenry; and 2. Different willingness to participate between individuals versus social organizations.

Australia, a country that joined the Alliance in 2015, opened a consultation period for the elaboration of the National Action Plan. A short notice published on the Web alerted that the government has not shown interest in publicizing such consultation period meant for public participation and that political and social organizations have not activated their members to contribute to this true opportunity to express their opinions to a plan whose central objective is to gather such opinions (Williams, 2016). The author complained the low diversity of those organizations that participated and that, up to that date (March 13th, 2016), only 24 citizens had shown interest in editing the National Action Plan of that country. She also complains about the lack of participation of political parties, think tanks, guilds and the Australian Council for the Social Sciences. Summarizing, this notice exhibits the lack of interest by the government and by the main political organizations to involve the common citizen in promoting possible changes in the government's operation, which is precisely contrary to the central goal of the OGP alliance. One may wonder: What would have happened if the consultation period, instead of being directed to *social organizations*, would have been directed to Australians as *individuals*?

An answer to this query may be deduced or derived from the experiment made in Ireland under the auspices of the CIMULACT project. The purpose of this project is to analyze the relevance that research and innovation has for countries of the European Union, by including the opinion of citizens and by validating needs and requests coming from society. The project acts with the conviction that collective intelligence gives Europe the competitive advantage that may be derived from the relevance of its research (Warnke, 2016).

A meeting of citizens that were expected to represent the diversity of the country's population in terms of age, gender, education, occupation and wish to contribute was organized in Ireland. The invitation was done through the Web and national press. One hundred and sixty-four citizens showed interest and forty-five were selected. In spite that the subject to be considered was very specific, that the meeting would take place on a fixed date and place, which introduced limitations of time and travel, and that the motivation had to be sent in writing to the organizers, the number of citizens that expressed a desire to attend exceeded the capacity of the place selected for the meeting (Fitzgerald et al., 2016). It seems clear that citizens are desirous to express themselves, when the opportunity is offered. I would also expect that attracting *individuals*, with preference to *social organizations* and by using government activities as discussion themes, in a continuous process as described for the Inclusive Power, the citizen participation is ensured, for Australia and other countries.

Canada has joined the Alliance in 2012 and is one of the nations that advanced most in its National Plan of Action. The plan encompasses three areas: Information, data and dialogue. *Data* refers to crude data produced by research, that may be published, shared and used to increase collective knowledge and for the creation of ways for public and private innovation. *Information* refers to information management (study and interpretation of data), that has not been published for national security reasons and because of traditional practices to keep it covert or secret. *Dialog* refers to the direct participation of citizens in government. While there have been advances in publications of raw data that belong to the government, there has not been any significant improvement in dialog with citizens nor in publication of information and data management. The meager advances in these two areas are due to critical tensions between structures of the traditional government and its culture, on one side, and conceptions of a more participative government on the other side. The most important conclusion is that, in order for dialogue to take place the bureaucratic structures of government have to be changed (Roy, 2016).

Roy's conclusion is interesting and points in the right direction, but it does not tackle the way to get there. It is clear that the present state of affairs, wherever it may be, either does not want or is unable to substantially change itself; if that were not the case, changes would already have taken place. What has been proposed here is a change in the *power structure* of government by introducing another *independent power* with the capability of commanding and promoting the changes that citizenry sees fit. That power is the Inclusive Power.

After presenting some ideas related to the opportunities of using collective intelligence to solve political problems I invite the reader to do the following exercise with data of his/her government: 1. Prepare a list of the names of those institutions that have the rank of Ministry or equivalent of the Executive, Legislative and Judiciary Powers; 2.

Include in that list the corresponding annual budget or the money spent by each institution the past year; and 3. Grade each institution of the list with a number— from 0 to 10, for example—according to its performance (a) and importance (b) for the solution of those problems that *you* perceive in your society. I hope that you will be glad of having it done, that you will get some new ideas to comment with your surroundings and, perhaps, to support to the insertion of the Inclusive Power in your government.

After having determined the MHGRs, the Inclusive Power will probably wish to determine roughly the limits of responsibilities that it expects government to take upon itself, for each MHGR. For example, if the specific MHGR is Education or Learning, it should be known what is understood by high-quality education, equality, social inclusion, all levels, research, curriculum content, private and public sector, government (federal, national, state, municipal, etc.), which are some of the terms used in the description of purposes and goals of ministries with that name. I believe that effort should be dedicated to specifying goals, responsibilities and costs. It is a task of the corresponding Ministry to present a diagnosis of the present situation and a proposal for changes. The Inclusive Power, with that proposal, will start a public discussion and give its opinions over time, as these are found to be representative or have considerable support. A similar procedure would be useful for each Ministry.

Concurrently, the Inclusive Power will stand ready to receive from citizens proposals for discussion on subjects of their interest, regarding government and society in general. This activity includes overseeing activities of *all* powers of the State.

Inclusive Power should be capable of maintaining a harmonious relationship between individuals, society and government. It should also gather enough wisdom to prevent formation and/or confrontation between such factions described by Priestland as "castes" that attempt to lead and control society (Priestland, 2013; see p. 21). This should not be difficult to achieve since the *entire society* is constantly involved through this Power.

The advantages that the insertion of Inclusive Power into a government structure signify makes that adoption urgent; society pays dearly for each day that goes by without being able to make use of them.

The Will of the People

After having pointed out advantages of an adoption of the Inclusive Power and, especially, the reticence of governments to initiate or allow structural changes, something should be said about the possibilities to achieve such adoption. It will not happen spontaneously, it will have to be imposed through political strength.

The only visible political force outside government, with enough strength for an imposition, is the Will of the People. But such will does not commonly exist, it has to be developed, formulated and felt by the People before attempting an imposition.

History shows at least two good examples of the People's egalitarian capacity to concentrate both its collective intelligence and sufficient force to impose the People's will: The insurrection of 508 B.C., in Athens, and the French Revolution.

Both struggles illustrate four characteristics for their success. These are (Hallward, 2018):

1. Capacity to gather together the supporting members, and to formulate and maintain a common purpose or general will;
2. Individual members appear simply as minimally differentiated as part of the collective (no distinguishable or dominating leaders);
3. People that assemble in support of the project are capable to quickly move to find ways to prevail over opposing forces, even using quasi-military forces;
4. Success in the struggle enables the victor to impose a government that can execute its demands.

These four characteristics are difficult to assemble, and they come accompanied with the high risk of considerable bloodshed, which makes their ways not to be recommended. However, lately, social and technical changes have occurred, which may allow similar results to be obtained by peaceful forceful political means.

The resistance of a government to a change that has very strong popular support may be weakened and defeated. If the reasons for its resistance are worthless or obnoxious as to rouse moral indignation, many politicians will be quick to get on the right side. Pertinent questions that demand answers and discussion posed on the Web could increase adherents to the cause. Those questions could be of the type: Why doesn't the government (or a party or an individual) want to hear the direct opinion of the People? Do the People have the right to freely express their opinions? Do you think that the opinions of the People are not worth of attention? Do you not want to know why the government (political party, President, Congress, Senate, the Judiciary, etc.) has an approval of barely 30 per cent? Should the citizen keep paying taxes when he has no say on how the money will be spent? Do you believe the government can be improved? The use of social media on the Web should be useful and eventually give results: These will consist of a constitutional amendment adopting the Inclusive Power.

A more difficult situation develops in countries that, in their Constitution or traditions, equal political rights are not legally recognized for all citizens, or the Golden Rule and the principle of reciprocity cannot be applied. This situation is not exotic, it occurs in countries whose government's structure or purpose is determined by the preservation of a lineage, an ideology, a theocracy, a colony-like relationship with another country, et cetera. As examples, the difficulty or desirability of introducing an Inclusive Power into the Islamic Republic of Iran, the Kingdom of Lesotho and the Vatican City State can be readily detected.

Organization and Operation

Every power, be it of new introduction or with historical heritage, must have defined purposes, expressed responsibilities, a basic organizational structure, operating rules, and a procedure to choose its principals and their legal terms in office.

In the case of the Inclusive Power (IP) of a country, due to its very nature, it has to be the citizenry who determines what it expects from that power. The results of such a determination will be different for each country. Some ideas will be presented here to illustrate how this author visualizes the successful adoption of an IP by a country, by mentioning those items that he considers of essential attention. There is no intention to deal with legalities, the idea is simply to help the reader and citizenry in their pondering if the adoption of IP may be advantageous in their cases.

Limitation to the New Power

The introduction of an IP is designed to be *the current and direct voice of the People*, as distinguished from postures, actions or omissions of elected representatives. IP is an integral part of government. As an independent power it must work with the rest of independent powers for the achievement of common goals. It, of course, has to achieve goals that are of its exclusive responsibility.

Common objectives have to do with the wellbeing of society, opportunities, progress, stability and relations with other societies. It should be recalled at this point that there is indisputable evidence that the majority of the world population does not approve or is dissatisfied with the performance of their governments (see Table 4, p. 35). This fact makes it necessary to differentiate the current opinion of the People from the expressions of spokesmen of other powers or other entities or individuals which try to usurp the power to speak on their behalf. The voice of the People is expressed by the Rapporteur of the IP. When done by another person, if he/she wishes to be legal and precise, will have to do it by repeating what the Rapporteur has expressed, mentioning the date at which it was originally done. As an example: When Congress, Senate, Assembly or equivalents, have prepared and enacted laws, as representatives or agents of the People, they should be aware that if such laws, after having been discussed through the IP, are found not to be acceptable by the People, the People will express such fact through the Rapporteur.

Goals that are the exclusive responsibility of the IP are: 1. Receive and activate discussions of matters proposed by any citizen and related to his country's society; 2. Preserve all contents of discussions; 3.

Publish through the Web, progresses made on all discussions; 4. Request from other powers information required to aid or advance current discussions; 5. When a discussion reaches a stable result, determine which conclusions or alternatives have enough support to merit a citizens' proposal before whoever should act on them; 6. Submit for discussion to the IP reasoned subject matters requested by other independent powers of Government; 7. Prepare technical reports on results obtained from the most relevant discussions that take place within the system; 8. Preserve and amplify the communication system between citizens, in order to include as many citizens as viable; 9. Channel Recall Referendums for any government official, when requested by the citizens of the corresponding jurisdiction (national, state or municipal). Such referendums are to be organized and decided with urgency; and 10. Serve as a constant promoter of opportunities for a better society and happier citizens.

Operation and decision taking by the citizenry within the IP are complex processes, likely to take a long time (although some may be very quick), because many people are involved. Those decisions or actions carry the weight of knowledge, desires and preferences of the whole population; they are products of collective intelligence. It would be very strange if they should not be good decisions (Landemore, 2014a; 2014b). However, the possibility exists, that the person or entity affected, may want to contribute important information that has not been considered. In that case the IP will make such information public and ask for a revision of the decision.

Structure of the Inclusive Power

Functions assigned to the IP can be carried out by a simple structure, with few managers, a limited number of support staff and a population willing to express itself. This implies a much smaller budget than that of the rest of independent powers and, at the same time, a contribution with a great social and economic significance.

The structure is envisioned with three executive positions; 1. Rapporteur; 2. Vice-Rapporteur; and 3. Director of the System. The Rapporteur is the main representative of the IP, in a similar way in which the President is the main representative of the Executive Power; the Vice-Rapporteur assists him and substitutes him in his absence. These positions are named *Rapporteurs* because they recount or repeat the voice of the People; it is the way to highlight that are not representatives of the People, they are their spokespersons. The Director of the System has the responsibility to adopt or develop computer programs and operations that receive citizens' contributions, and to improve and adjust them to the changing needs; to supervise operations in the whole country; to create and distribute instruction materials for the use of the system; and to prepare technical reports related to the information received and decisions taken.

Election of Executives

Since the IP is the voice of the People, its executives, Rapporteur, Vice-Rapporteur and Director of the System must be elected by the same citizens that have the right to vote for the President of the Executive Power or equivalents. In the absence of such a structure, they may be elected by all members of society that have reached voting age.

The author's preferred procedure to take care of this election includes the acceptance of all candidates that are willing to accept the post. Each candidate will make himself or herself be known through two summaries of no more than 1000 words each. The first one will contain personal data: Profession or occupation, experience, health and publications. The second one will contain his or her ideas about the purpose, usefulness and relevance of the IP. The summaries will be distributed through the Web and other media; such publication will substitute for proselytizing campaigns. There will be two elections: One for Rapporteur and Vice-Rapporteur, and another one for the Director of the System. The candidate that gets more votes in the first one will be declared or sworn in as Rapporteur, and the one that follows in number of votes will be declared Vice-Rapporteur. The election for the Director of the System takes place concurrently but separately from the just-mentioned because the position requires experience and technical and scientific knowledge of communication, information and computing. The person that gets more votes will be declared Director of the System. These executive positions will have an office term of five years with no reelection allowed.

Individuals in these executive positions may be removed through recall referendum, initiated by any citizen, as any other discussion topic, evaluated for adequate citizens' support, and presented to the national electoral authority by any one of the three executive positions which are not being subjected to recall referendum. If all three executive positions are being subjected to recall referendums at the same time, they will be processed in the order: 1. Rapporteur, 2. Vice-Rapporteur and 3. Director of the System.

Administration of the Inclusive Power

IP will prepare a yearly working plan and operating budget, just as the rest of the independent powers of government. During this process IP will consider suggestions from citizens. Each semester the Rapporteur will publish through the Web a summary of results obtained in the past six months. At the end of each year of activities he/she will give an oral public presentation that includes the goals achieved and not achieved during the year, with graphic and quantitative support, outlining the significance of what has been accomplished. The full report will be published through the Web.

The IP will use the Open-Book system to report its monthly expenditure, with the same detail used by internal administrative files, fifteen days after the end of the month (Case, 1996). It will include the possibility of inquiring clarification of specific payments and to get answers through the Web; answers will be given during the next thirty days after the inquiry took place.

The adoption of this procedure is suggested on the basis of the excellent results it has produced under a variety of circumstances, including the refinement of social trust as prompt answers are obtained from government offices (NCEO, 2017; Jeffco, CO. Public Schools, 2014; Pasquali, 2014b; Fort Collins, 2017). The practice of this procedure, in governments that have not had experience with it, may be valuable for the study of its general acceptance.

System Usage

The purpose of the information-discussion system of the IP is the exchange of ideas between many individuals. The largest group is made up by all citizens of the nation. Additionally, citizens will be divided into subgroups that represent political administrative jurisdictions, such as State, County and Municipality, in order to allow and expedite discussions on issues of local interest with the use of the same system. It will also be possible to allow contributions from anyone allowed into the system by requiring that, during the quantitative determination of popular support for a legal or administrative action, only people belonging to the specific jurisdiction participate.

Participation of a large number of people requires assurance that information received and made public, be done respectfully, with proper terms for any age and limited to contents that comply with human rights accepted by the United Nations. These conditions are routinely applied by the majority of known social networks. An example of such conditions, among many that could serve as a guide, is the Code of Ethics of the Yoinfluyo Foundation (2017). The system will be able to detect breach of rules and will inform, whoever attempted it, the reason for not publishing his/her contribution.

Special care will be used during the quantitative evaluation of support or rejection to conclusions that may be transformed into IP's requests, suggestions or recommendations to the other independent powers or the whole society. This means that each citizen legally authorized to give his/her opinion on a specific issue, be it of municipal, state or national, has to be registered as such, have an individual access password that will not allow other people to express his/her opinion or change it. The electoral and civil registries will attend to the reliability of the system. Before formal quantitative evaluations of support are executed, tendencies as discussions advance, may be followed through quick, low-cost polls directed to the stakeholder population within the nation.

The system will also have on its website examples on how to propose a subject for discussion, how to contribute to it, present evidence, literature and personal experience, ask questions, give examples, use appropriate and respectful language et cetera. This same information can also be shown on TV programs, taught at public schools and demonstrated at public libraries with Web access.

Fictional Discussion

I thought it entertaining to imagine how the discussion of a topic would take place where one hundred million people participate, freely and concurrently. This is what I have proposed as a good way for people to learn what others think, add their thoughts, and appreciate how knowledge and ideas evolve as the discussion goes forward. Contribution will be made by individuals, not by organizations, and only ideas or quantities will be part of the discussions: No names of the contributors. It will be a collegial discussion—where everyone has the same standing as anyone else.

I have chosen a topic for discussion. Since I hope that many people will read the book, I looked for a subject that would have a high visibility, so that most people in the world would have had the opportunity to hear that such a topic exists. No special knowledge would be needed to join in. The topic is: The Building of the Wall on the border between the United States of America and the Republic of Mexico.

Let us assume that the discussion takes place through the Web using a system similar to the one described for the use of the Inclusive Power. To be of real interest, the discussion would have to take place either in the USA or in Mexico. Since the idea was initiated in the USA, let us suppose that it will take place there—for now. The population of the USA is approximately 325 million (2017) and the number of voters has reached 200 million in 2016. There would be around 200 million people with the right to enter the discussion of the topic. Since many people with such right do not comply, let us suppose that only 100 million have a genuine interest to enter the discussion. Let us also suppose that all 100 million voters are or will become familiar with the system and are able to clearly express their opinion, ask questions, contribute information, dispute the truth of statements made by others and differentiate between opinions, facts and imagination.

In the first few days of the discussion I expect a group of opinions on *what* should be done: To build it, not to build it, to make it with bricks, to make a fence—not a wall, to make it high, to make it low so that most animals can clear it, and so on. There are so many people with access to the system that, at the beginning, a specific opinion or one very much similar to it, will be received many times; they all shall be treated as one. That procedure should keep opinions to a low number, say 50. Those opinions should be enough to advance in other directions, into *how*, *why* or *what for* and *when*.

The why and what for would probably widen the discussion. The wall was proposed originally for security issues related to the southern border. Each person has his/her concept of security. That fact will foster the introduction of a series of components of security: The illegal entry of any migrant, the illegal entry of drugs, the illegal crossing of migrants—entry and exit—related to drug distribution, the entry of migrants who may turn out to be criminals or are known to be criminals or terrorists, and the entry of numerous people that are willing to take the risks of deportation in order to better their lives' conditions.

The why and what for will also produce some ramifications, such as: What about the security related to the rest of the borders—northern, Pacific coast, Atlantic coast, Caribbean coast and the sky? What are the advantages and disadvantages of having a wall or a fence that allows seeing what is on the other side? For each type of wall or fence, what are the construction, maintenance, operating and predictable effectiveness for the different purposes? Are there other more effective or as effective ways to get the desired results, at lower cost? How would the wall or fence stop the introduction of drugs when drones can be used to transport them to places far from it? These questions would probably induce 50 more items to be considered.

In another direction, some citizens would wish to know how the present situation has developed. Most of the issues that have been mentioned have been related to illegal actions. This means that there are laws and that they have been broken. Are these laws adequate, inadequate or insufficient? If this should be part of the problem, it would involve the past and present attention of Congress. If current laws are adequate, part of the problem has been the unwillingness or lack of capacity to uphold them; in such case there would be illegal migrants and also willing or unwilling, direct or indirect accessories. Could it also be that there are conflicts between existing laws or existing principles? For example: If an illegal immigrant woman marries an illegal immigrant man and gives birth to a child at a hospital in the USA, the child acquires the right to be a USA citizen by birth. If the illegal migrant condition of his or her parents is discovered, and they are legally deported without the child, would the law be creating what may be called an artificial orphan? These questions would probably induce 20 more items to be considered.

Krogstad et al. (2017) published the number of illegal immigrants in the USA from 1990 to 2016. Their data are derived from population surveys. The number for year 1990 is 3.5 million; for 2000 is 8.6 million; for 2009 is 11.3 million; for 2015 is 11 million; and for 2016 is 11.3 million. The data indicate that the topic has seen action for a long time. The discussion, at some point, will touch upon what causes the desire to migrate to the United States legally or illegally. Such desire may vary according to the different types of people that the USA may receive. If the causes of that desire do not change—which means conditions of individuals in other countries and conditions in the USA—a good wall or a good fence will probably be a partial and temporary solution at best.

The consideration of the desires of migrants to emigrate to the USA has to be matched with the desire of the USA to receive them. The decision on a migration policy requires the determination of, at least, the following types of migrants that the USA considers should be accepted or not accepted, according to its Constitutional principles, the law and national interest: 1. People that are to be attracted and invited; 2. People that would be useful, if not necessary, for the economy or other areas; 3. People that, because of family close ties, would protect the family structure; 4. People that may want or need protection from dangers or persecution; 5. People that are not wanted because their past behavior indicates unsuitability for a well-behaved social life; 6. People that are not wanted because they have acted as enemies of the USA or may have terrorist tendencies; and 7. People that, at entry, will be put under custody, because they have pending serious legal charges. The discussion would probably include a detailed examination of the current policy to look for possible improvements.

As the discussion advances, quantitative data related to the building of the wall and the different aspects of the migration process, will have to be clarified. Different sources declare or publish different numbers for the same situation or process. These differences are found even between specialized research institutions that deal with this topic. To develop a meaningful comparison between points of view there needs to be an agreement on the facts involved. In some cases, it may be necessary to do research to fill some critical gaps.

At some point, the recognition of two very different sets of circumstances to be discussed will take place: 1. An established 11.3-million group of illegal immigrants, and 2. The creation of an immigration policy that will reflect an effective adjustment to present and foreseeable conditions.

All aspects of this complex and multifaceted topic will be analyzed, studied and debated by those 100 million people who have an interest and the desire to contribute. With the enormous amount of knowledge, brain power and time dedicated to this topic, several acceptable alternatives for actions, policies and regulations, for next year and following decades, will be surely produced.

The topic will have been discussed, thought through and evaluated by the most diverse, interested and knowledgeable group available in the country: At little cost and associated with much personal satisfaction. I believe the results would be a true expression of a nation, well above the results obtainable by partisan discussions.

What Is Going On

When considering the adoption of the Inclusive Power by a government it is wise to be conscious of the effects that the current research in the field of Artificial Intelligence (AI) is likely to produce. AI is a field of intensive competition and collaboration in academia, the private sector and governments. AI, among other things, deals with the creation and use of computer systems that are capable to use knowledge obtainable through the Web and skillfully manage it to solve very complex problems.

One of the areas of AI is global-engineering-connected intelligence. Associated with the use of the Web, it consists of the production of artifacts with a practical purpose (Tekinerdogan, 2017). Through it, knowledge on any subject may be used, discussed and shared by all in solving many types of problems, including those of the social areas. According to expected advances, the destiny of a society will depend greatly on the ability with which its people will make use of these new methods.

I am going to illustrate with a simple example the type of economic analyses that will probably become almost instantaneous and commonplace, in dealing with a prospect around the globe. It may be done by any person with free access to the Web. The object of such analyses is not limited to the field of economics, it could indistinctly be related to the sciences, humanities, technology or combinations of them, given the appropriate data and computing programs. Serrano et al. (2017) give a recent account of the building of what they call the Next Generation Internet. The reader may envision examples, situations or problems as complex as desired.

Let us suppose that you have learned that, for a recipe that you wish to try out, you will need mango vinegar. You look on the Web if the stores close to your home carry the product and learn that they do not. With a wider search on the Web you locate many varieties and many sources. Prices fall into a range of 2 to 3 US$ per ounce; a liter would cost between 70 and 106 US$. Initially you are shocked and conclude that the recipe can be experimented with another type of vinegar. After a while you decide that the production of mango vinegar may be the type of business that can solve your financial problems and opt to research how to deal with it and take the following actions:

1. Learn what countries and areas produce mangoes, varieties, prices and who controls the business.
2. Learn the process by which the vinegar is produced, who are the producers, what equipment is generally used, its cost and the employees needed to operate it.
3. Learn if the current mango production is sufficient and can be counted on, or if it is necessary to establish a crop or finance one.
4. Learn which mango varieties are used for vinegar production, agronomic conditions and typical yields.

5. For each of the potential areas, learn the legal requirements for nationals and foreigners. Study the social stability and the rule of law in each of the countries being considered.

After studying the results of the first five actions you conclude that it is feasible to produce one liter of mango vinegar of good quality at a cost of between 5 and 10 US dollars. This result encourages you to look further and estimate the following:

6. The advantage of producing vinegar in a mango-producing country or in countries that are good consumers. Learn about taxes and costs (transportation, customs, distribution and storage).
7. Find, for the best conditions encountered, the required investment to develop the project.

You found that the investment has to be of tens of millions of US dollars with an estimated annual benefit of around 32 per cent. Since you may barely be able to dream about that amount of money, you apply to banks for financing. You write up the project with all the data that economists, at the banks where you ask for a loan, require considering if your project should be approved, and under what conditions. Banks will provide you with the appropriate forms to be filled out. You have done so, but you have not turned them in yet.

A doubt invades you; you know that your interest in the mango vinegar business happened by chance.

You have invested four hours to obtain the necessary information and four hours to fill out the forms for the banks. You ask yourself: Could there be other projects that are more favorable? You like to live and work in contact with nature. How would a project that deals with ecological tourism in the basin of the Orinoco River or the Amazon River compare with the mango vinegar production? You will have to invest eight more hours to find out.

The fact that any person may be able to analyze and compare advantages of possible simple projects at the global level, in a few hours, determines the high probability that in the near future a race will take place for the search and control of the best possible projects—big, small, simple and complex—which will be accompanied by the displacement of existing projects and businesses that are less efficient. It seems that starters could become dominant.

The enormous quantity of information that may be obtained from the Web in a short time and the possibility to employ it using Artificial Intelligence shows the opportunity of solving very complex problems as they arise. I thought that one such a problem could be: *Alternative settings for the achievement of full and stable employment, in a country's competitive economy.* AI includes the interaction of mathematics, computer science, linguistics, philosophy, neurology and artificial psychology (Tekinerdogan, 2017).

FuturICT, a project initiated by the European Union, to be executed in a period of ten years and a budget of one billion (10^9) Euros, serves to illustrate the types of results expected from the use of AI in the coming years. FuturICT is supported by the work of hundreds of European researchers for the development of new methods to integrate scientific models, data and concepts. In order to increase research capabilities, the project fosters regional input and programs to add young researchers (Bishop and Helbing, 2017; Helbing and Bishop, 2017).

Data needed to obtain specific solutions and predictions with these new methods will be provided by an associated project called Planetary Nervous System (NervousNet). It may be considered as a framework of sensors that send technologic, scientific and social data collected from the whole Earth—continually.

Results achieved by FuturICT will be shared with citizens, companies and other organizations. Currently—2018—two regions and 25 countries are associated with the project. Its size, the number of researchers and countries involved, are clear indications of the advantages expected from the use of the results obtained through the project.

It is not difficult to forecast consequences derived from this type of project. Countries that have access to results as they are produced will increase productivity and lower production costs, will increase the quality and coverage of social services, such as health care and will develop and adopt an education system of high quality and equity (in case they do not already have it). This, in turn, will place them in a favorable position in dealing with countries that have no access to those results or that are not able to use them. As a result of large differences in living conditions between countries, multiple and massive migrations are to be expected, together with the instabilities and sufferings that accompany them.

It is evident, for the good of all, that each country should prepare its government and population for the scenarios that are in the making.

To Be Taken into Account

In order to visualize the opportunities and difficulties that accompany the adoption of the Inclusive Power (IP) by a government of a country it is also useful to consider the following points: 1. The confidence that such an adoption could mean an improvement as related to the present; 2. The current conditions of the country allow for a successful adoption or if some experimentation is required; 3. The expected efficiency of discussions through the Web to achieve good decisions; and 4. The consequences of not adopting the IP.

The confidence that the introduction of the IP would mean an improvement could be built, as a start, through the study of its characteristics as presented in this book, accompanied by modifications suited to the specific country. A public discussion of the subject and the statistical weight of the resulting opinions will indicate if there is enough confidence or not. At a given time there may be doubts that indicate the need to see how countries that have adopted the IP are doing.

Characteristics of the country that is considering the adoption of the IP that may be related to that change are: 1. Model on which the Constitution has been written; 2. Presence of populations that use different languages; and 3. Use or coverage area of the Web by the population. In countries where the Constitution must be framed by rigid precepts, religious or of any other nature, the adoption of an IP is difficult to achieve. In such cases, perhaps, it would be possible to adopt a system in which subject matters to be discussed are limited by the current government. The system would not be a power, but a point of reference. Some examples of countries that could be in such a situation would be Iran, North Korea, Saudi Arabia and Vatican City.

Some countries with great territories such as China and India have several "nations" (regions or states) with different languages within the country. Discussions that would take place within the system used by the IP would suffer limitations by the lack of mastery in a common language. In these cases, the adoption of a system that accepts only government matters of local interest may be considered.

Decisions taken in each region could be presented to the rest of the country to test the convenience of extending their adoption to other regions. Alternatively, a quick and accurate translation arrangement may be more practical and unifying.

The literature offers examples of effective Web discussions where many people participate in the achievement of acceptable decisions of good quality (Iandoli et al., 2017; and references therein). These authors also present a way to organize such discussions.

Of considerable interest and pertinence is the impact that the introduction of political blogs has had in Malaysia, where they probably had a determinant role in the victory of the opposition political party in the 2008 election. In this country, political activity done with the use of blogs, has increased the direct participation of the citizenry. It has allowed daily exchanges of information and opinions, without censorship and outside the scope of political parties (Hakim et al., 2017). This political activity and its effects, that took place in a country with a population of 30 million people, is a clear demonstration that the participation system proposed here is feasible and effective.

Working in another direction, researchers have tried to find out why, well-established massive Web communication systems—as Facebook and Twitter—on many occasions, have not been useful to political activists in maintaining important socially-important issues alive for enough time to mobilize the masses. Even on those occasions in which they have been successful, it has been difficult for them to activate politicians, institutions and society in general. *Coordinated collective interaction* is essential for the use of collective intelligence in taking decisions by society.

Cebrian et al. (2016) concluded that systems such as Facebook have been designed to call the attention of the masses but are not effective to engage the public with a cause. To engage individuals with a project it is necessary to discover and use a *structure of incentives* that will create interpersonal motivation, which leads to collective decision and action.

This observation could explain how the efforts to get citizens' participation in political matters have not been successful in Australia, where mostly *organizations* were invited, but hardly *individuals*; while success has been achieved in Malaysia and Ireland, where *individuals* had personal incentives to receive information and to contribute opinions. Organizations do not seem to be able to create or foster interpersonal motivation when the matter under consideration is related to the organization's objectives but not related to general objectives of society.

The structure of incentives advanced by Cebrian et al. (2016) is spontaneously included in the natural right and duty, felt by every citizen, to participate collectively in the creation of a powerful voice to help build and supervise government.

CONCLUSIONS

"The great aim of education is not knowledge but action."
Herbert Spencer

"Knowledge has no value unless you put it to practice."
Anton Chekhov

"Your assumptions are your windows on the world. Scrub them off every once in a while, or the light won't come in."
Isaac Asimov

"Communication leads to community, that is, to understanding, intimacy and mutual valuing."
Rollo May

Introduction

This chapter is dedicated to the summary of the main conclusions that have been reached through the book. Some are clearly stated in the text, while others are of a more general nature and have been derived by combining ideas presented in different chapters and from the cited literature.

Conclusions are ordered in such a way that the reader can perceive a sequence of building blocks that result in a government structure that will be able to adjust and keep pace with the changes that the population requires.

List of Conclusions

1. Society is drenched through with the notion that politics is not practiced by good people, and that we should stay away from it. It is a notion opposite to the ideas of Ancient Greeks' proper democratic behavior, where citizens that kept to themselves and did not get involved into politics and social matters were contemptuously called "idiots."

2. It is worthwhile to dedicate efforts to improve your society and the operation of its government.

3. Through history government has been controlled by three small groups: Sages and priests, merchants, aristocrats and soldiers; with the notable exceptions of democracies, such as that of Athens in Ancient Greece.

4. The success of these democracies was rooted in the direct participation of all citizens and enjoyed general support.

5. Man, as a species, has reached a dominant position on Earth because of curiosity, power of observation and interpretation, ability to communicate, create ways to concentrate and store findings in numerous ways.

6. The United Nations serves as a point of reference, for the determination of accepted human rights that are to be protected by governments, and for the collection of data that reflect how each of them is complying. The United Nation operates through decisions of governments of nations; they do not directly represent populations.

7. Protection and compliance of Human Rights in countries and regions is observed, measured and studied by many organizations by using indices: Democratic Index, Democracy Ranking, Liberty in the World, Freedom of the Press, Free Access to Internet, Human Rights compliance, Corruption Index, Homicide Rate, Government Approval by citizens, Happiness Index et cetera. Results of these studies are published.

8. The global evaluation of governments, using indices just mentioned above, paints a very troublesome situation for man in society, which is in dire of attention: More than half of the human population is tolerating governments that do not have its approval!

9. To advocate changes that would lead to the free expression of human capacities and opportunities for citizens' participation in the deliberation process is a promising way to effectively amend the present state of affairs.

10. The fact that some governments operate much better than others is an indication that improvement is possible and ways to achieve it are known.

11. Inherent to social life is the evaluation and comparison between the advantages of life in society versus limitations society imposes on the individual. These limitations are legally managed and enforced by government.

12. Two strong and concurrent collective forces are in operation within a society: One molds the person into a member through customs, language, history, legends, laws, regulation, music, flags and surroundings. The mold represents the past and most of the present.

    The second force develops through new knowledge, changes in the social framework, imitation of other societies, lack of liberties and oppression by authorities, very difficult economic circumstances or any condition that has changed or is changing quickly. The second force represents part of the present and the possibility to shape the future. It gains strength and becomes dominant with communication between citizens which, in turn, leads to changes. While the first force is unfaltering and stagnant, the second one usually acts in pulses; very rarely does it act steadily.

13. There is a lot at stake in the appropriate development of the individual for his physical and mental health, happiness, capacity to learn, and his contribution to society of the current and that of following generations.
Two critical stages that require attention and care stand out: The first 1000 days from conception, and the period during which decisions and/or sexual activities lead to the bearing of children. Their appropriate development is favored by parents that are conscious of their duties and practice sexual responsibility.

14. Poverty or low socioeconomic status has many adverse effects on the development of children and adults. The social context in which families develop determines the outcome of children's lives and the transmittal of unfavorable environments from generation to the next.

15. Societies, climates and knowledge change with time. Adaptation to the new conditions is the natural response. Governments change very little: Bureaucracies, power structures, ideologies, and pre-existing conceptions are obstacles to the free search of alternatives needed for adaptation.

16. Most governments have retained a structure that was built for a different society of the past. Such structures are inefficient and obsolescent.

17. The system composed of the Executive-Legislative-Judiciary Powers, under the sole supervision by the media as an expression of the population is obsolete. It results in power being controlled by political parties and other groups (with force or funds). A new system where a new independent power that is propelled by the collective intelligence of all citizens, who will take the command of the government's direction and be the guard of its loyal operation is in order.

18. When collectively dealing with the unknown, the participation of all—where none has different rights from the rest—is still the simplest, quickest and more intelligent way to reach the best political decisions.

One can plainly see that this is not the way political decisions are being made. They are taken by political parties, bureaucracy, elected officials and special-interest groups. This means that, at any one time, they are not the best political decisions.

19. Political decisions of high rank, such as political system, missions and responsibilities of government, changes to the Constitution, oversight and evaluation of government's operation, should be taken on the basis of collective deliberations of citizens, or receive such a collective approval.

20. No current government has a structure that organizes collective deliberations of all citizens or gives political power to such deliberations. To correct such deficiency, a new independent Constitutional power called Inclusive Power is proposed and delineated.

21. The Inclusive Power will ensure for society: A government where the authorized collective voice will be heard and taken into account, the capability to detect and make the necessary adjustments to new conditions, a continuous flow of information, ideas and suggestions that will increase the political knowledge of the population, and citizens that feel they are part of a collegial unity; where authority and power is shared equally among colleagues.

22. The unification derived from the recognition and accord between many diverse individuals is immensely happier than one that is derived from the imposition of uniformity.

23. The adoption by many countries of the new government model, promises, not only to increase the wellbeing for the population of each country, but also to improve the relationships among countries and the related reduction of probabilities of war.

24. The current dominant form of government is based on power concentration and operates without direction or supervision from the People. The direction and supervision of government is best achieved with the

collective intelligence of the People. The upgrading to such a new government model, in many cases, can be achieved swiftly, peacefully and profitably.

25. **Inclusive Power will establish the impact of timely adjustment**. Desirable changes will be discovered by anyone; thereafter discussed and accorded among members of society. Needed adjustments or repairs will be introduced timely, naturally and peacefully—without obstruction. When government and society are kept in optimal conditions they will allow the best possible conditions for wellbeing and happiness.

REFERENCES

"Those who have knowledge do not predict. Those who predict do not have knowledge."
Lao Tzu

"Beware of false knowledge it is more dangerous than ignorance."
George Bernard Shaw

References mentioned in the text are listed in alphabetical order of the surname of the first author or the name or the initials of the publishing organization. They have been chosen with several purposes; some because they are essential to study a subject; others because they contain data related to some point in time and may not be valid for the date the book is being read, but the same source periodically updates the information, such may be the United Nations; other contain information that deals with points of view or data that the reader may want to review, because of their importance or antagonistic character. There are a few references in Spanish; the reader can use the program *Google Translate* to obtain an approximate translation to English that can be reached at the site (https://translate.google.com/). Some references are included directly in the text as links and are not listed here.

The Web site www.mentationpublication.com can be used to contact the author. In certain cases, he may be able to send the reader a document that is difficult to locate or obtain.

The list of references follows:

Adam, Frédéric, 2012, 20 years of decision making and decision support research published by the Journal of Systems: Journal of Decision Systems, v. 21, n. 2, p. 93-99

Alcalá, L.E., 2012, Las élites culposas: Caracas, Editorial Libros Marcados, 421 p.

Alcalá, L.E., 2017a, Mandar es preferible a protestar y exigir. See and hear: http://doctorpolitico.com/ (2017211)

Alcalá, L.E., 2017b, Referéndum Anual de la República (Republic's Yearly Referendum) See and hear: http://doctorpolitico.com/2017/09/23/referendum-anual-de-la-republica/

Aristóteles (384-322 a. d. J.C.), 1979, La Política: Bogotá, Editorial Didáctica, traducción de José Gregorio Neira C., 219 p.

Aristotle, 2013, Aristotle's Politics/translated and with an introduction, note, and glossary by Carnes Lord: Chicago, The University of Chicago Press, 265 p.

Atlee, Tom, 2012, Empowering public wisdom: Berkeley, Evo Editions, 256 p.

Baratta, Alessandro, 1990, Resocialización o control social: Lima, Seminario de Criminología Crítica y Sistema Penal, Comisión Andina de Juristas y la Comisión Episcopal de Acción Social, Lima, del 17 al 21 de Septiembre de 1990, 10 p.

Bater, Richard, 2011, Hope from below: composing the commons in Iceland: Open Democracy, 4 p. See: https://www.opendemocracy.net/richard-bater/hope-from-below-composing-commons-in-iceland

Bhutan, 2008, The Constitution of Bhutan, 75 p. ISBN 9993675407

Bishop, Steven, and Helbing, Dirk, 2017, FuturICT: Global computing for our complex world, 5 p.

Biswas-Diener, Robert, Diener, Ed, and Tamir, Maya, 2004, The psychology of subjective well-being: Daedalus, v. 133, n. 2, p. 18-25

Black, M.M., Walker, S.P., et al., 2017, Early childhood development coming of age: science through the life course: The Lancet, v. 389, January 7, 2017, p. 77.90

Boragina, G.S., 2016, Propiedad privada y pobreza. See: http://elrepublicanoliberalii.blogspot.com/2016/04/gabriel-s-boragina-propiedad-privada-y.html (2016426)

Britto, P.R., Lye, S.J., et al., 2017, Nurturing care: promoting early childhood development: The Lancet, v. 389, January 7, 2017, p. 91-102

Calas, Georges, 2017, Mineral resources and sustainable development: Elements, v. 13, n. 5, p. 301-306

Campbell, T.C., and Campbell, T.M., 2006, The China study: Dallas, Texas, BenBella Books, 417 p.

Campbell, T.C., y Campbell, T.M., 2012, El studio de China: Dallas, Texas, BenBella , 419 p.

Case, John, 1996, Open-book management. The coming business revolution: Harper Collins Publishers, 224 p.

Cebrian, Manuel, Rahwan, Iyad, and Pentlan, Alex, 2016, Beyond viral: Communications of the ACM, v. 59, n. 4, p. 36-39

Chandy, Laurence, 2017, No country left behind: The case for focusing greater attention on the world's poorest countries: Brookings Institution, Jan. 24, 2017, 11 p. See: https://www.brookings.edu/research/no-country-left-behind-the-case-for-focusing-greater-attention-on-the-worlds-poorest-countries/ (201736)

China, 2004, Constitution of the People's Republic of China. Preamble. See: http://www.npc.gov.cn/englishnpc/Constitution/2007-11/15/content_1372962.htm 2 p.

Chorodov, Frank, 1962, Out of step: New York, The Devin-Adair Company, 274 p.

Christensen, Tom, Lægreid, Per, Roness, P.G., and Røvik, K.A., 2007, Organization theory and the public sector: New York, Routledge, 208 p.

Cohen, L.J., 2011, The psychology of politics? Psychology Today, January 15, 2011, 5 p. See: https://www.psychologytoday.com/blog/handy-

psychology-answers/201101/the-psychology-politics
(2016614)

Coleman, J.S., 1988, Social capital in the creation of human capital: The American Journal of Sociology, v. 94, p. S95-S120

Crisp, Brian, 1994, Limitations to democracy in developing capitalist societies: The case of Venezuela: World Development, v. 22, n. 10, p. 1491-1509

Dettmer, Otto, 2010, The party's (largely) over: Political parties' membership is withering. That's bad news for governments, but not necessarily for democracy: The Economist, October 28th, 2010. See: http://www.economist.com/node/17306082 (2013328)

Edwards, Chris, 2016, Food subsidies: Downsizing Government, 15 p. (201694) See: http://www.downsizinggovernment.org/agriculture/food-subsidies

Eldersveld, S.J., 1964, Political parties: A behavioral analysis: Chicago, Rand McNally, 613 p.

Fauci, A.S., and Morens, D.M., 2016, Zika virus in the Americas—Yet another Arbovirus threat: The New England Journal of Medicine, v. 374, p. 601-604 See: http://www.nejm.org/doi/full/10.1056/NEJMp1600297?af=R&rss=currentIssue& (201738)

FFIS, 2013, Constitution of the Islamic Republic of Iran: Foundation for Iranian Studies. See: http://fis-iran.org/en/resources/legaldoc/constitutionislamic (2013919)

Fitzgerald, Ciara, McCarthy, Stephen, et al., 2016, Citizen participation in decision-making: can one make a difference? Journal of Decision Systems, v. 25—Sup 1, p. 248-260

Fort Collins, 2017, City of Fort Collins Open Book expenses. See: http://www.fcgov.com/openbook/?action=browse-expense-type (2017220)

Garbarino, James, 1998, Raising children in a socially toxic environment: Family Matters, N° 50, Winter 1998, p. 53-55

Gates, S.M., 2005, Organizing for reorganizing, in, Robert Klitgaard and Paul C. Light, eds.,High-performance government: Structure, leadership, Incentives: Rand Corporation, Chapter 5, p. 139-159

Georgiadis, Andreas, and Penny, M.E., 2017, Child undernutrition: opportunities beyond the first 1000 days: The Lancet Public Health, v. 2, n. 9, p e 399 See: http://www.sciencedirect.com/science/article/pii/S24682 66717301548 (2017102)

Goffman, Erving, 1961, Asylums. Essays on the social situation of mental patients and other inmates: New York, Doubleday & Company, 338 p.

Goffman, Erving, 2001, Internados: ensayos sobre la situación social de los enfermos mentales: Buenos Aires, Amorrortu, traducción del inglés de Goffman (1961) por María Antonia Oyuela de Grant. 189 p.

Grantham-McGregor, S.M., Fernald, L.C., and Sethuraman, Kavita, 1999, Effest of health and nutrition on cognitive and behavioural development in the first three years of life. Part 1: Low birth weight, breastfeeding, and protein-energy malnutrition: Food and Nutrition Bulletin, v. 20, n. 1, p. 52-75

Greger, Michael, and Stone, Gene, 2015, How not to die: New York, Flatiron Books, 562 p.

Greger, Michael, y Stone, Gene, 2016, Comer para no morir: Barcelona, Paidós, 676 p.

Guevara-A, Walter, 1989, Los militares en Bolivia: Nueva Sociedad, n. 56-57, p. 19-36

Hakim, A.A.A., Shuhidam, S.M., et al., 2017, An exploratory study on the impact of political blogs on citizen's participation in Malaysia political activism: The Social Sciences, v. 12, n. 1, p. 20-24 See: http://docsdrive.com/pdfs/medwelljournals/sscience/201 7/20-24.pdf (2017325)

Hallward, Peter, 2018, 'Concentration or representation: The struggle for popular sovereignty': Cogent Arts & Humanities, v. 4, 20 p.

Harden, B.J., 2004, Safety and stability for foster children: A developmental perspective: The Future of Children, v. 14, n. 1, p. 30-47

Helbing, Dirk, 2017, From remote-controlled to self-controlled citizens: The European Physical Journal Special Topics, 8 p. DOI: 10.1140/epjst/e2016-60372-1

Helbing, Dirk, and Bishop, Steven, 2017, FuturICT: Global computing for our complex world, 17 p.

Helliwell, John, Layard, Richard, and Sachs, Jeffrey, eds., 2012, World happiness report: Columbia University, The Earth Institute, 170 p. See: http://www.earth.columbia.edu/sitefiles/file/Sachs%20W riting/2012/World%20Happiness%20Report.pdf (201264)

Helliwell, John, Layard, Richard, and Sachs, Jeffrey, eds., 2013, World happiness report 2013: UN Sustainable Development Solutions Network (SDSN), 170 p. See: http://unsdsn.org/files/2013/09/WorldHappinessReport 2013_online.pdf (2013920)

Helliwell, John, Layard, Richard, and Sachs, Jeffrey, eds., 2016, World happiness report 2016, update volume I: Sustainable Development Solution Network, 70 p. See: http://worldhappiness.report/wp-content/uploads/sites/2/2016/03/HR-V1_web.pdf

Hess, A.E., and Frohlich, 2014, 12 countries that hate their government most: 24/7 Wall St., LLC, October 17, 2104, 4 p. See: http://247wallst.com/special-report/2014/10/17/12-countries-that-hate-their-government-most/ (201398)

Heywood, Andrew, 2012, Political ideologies: An introduction: Palgrave, Macmillan, 392 p.

Hong, Lu, and Page, S.E., 2004, Groups of diverse problem solvers can outperform groups of high-ability problem solvers: Proceedings of the National Academy of Sciences, v. 101, n. 46, p. 16385-16389

Horton, Richard, 2016a, The secrets of a healthy society: The Lancet, v. 387, January 23, 2016, p. 325

Horton, Richard, 2016b, The Rule of Law—an invisible determinant of health: The Lancet, v. 387, March 26, 2016, p. 1260

Horton, Richard, 2016c, Medicine and nutrition—"that's insane": The Lancet, v. 387, April 23, 2016, p.1706

HRW, 2015, World report 2015, events of 2014, 660 p. See: https://www.hrw.org/sites/default/files/world_report_do wnload/wr2015_web.pdf (2017226)

Hudson, John, and Küner, Stefan, 2016, Fairness for children: A league table of inequality in child-well-being in rich countries: UNICEF, Innocenti Report Card 13, 52 p.

Iandoli, Luca, Quinto, Ivana, et al., 2017, Supporting
    argumentation in online political debate: Evidence from an
    experiment of collective deliberation: New Media and
    Society, February 2017, 22 p. See:
    https://www.researchgate.net/profile/Mark_Klein/public
    ation/313546329_Supporting_argumentation_in_online_
    political_debate_Evidence_from_an_experiment_of_coll
    ective_deliberation/links/58a25f3592851c7fb4c1c5ea/Sup
    porting-argumentation-in-online-political-debate-
    Evidence-from-an-experiment-of-collective-
    deliberation.pdf (2017317)
Infobae, 2015, El Chavismo duplicó el número de empleados.
    See: http://www.infobae.com/2015/06/17/1735856-el-
    chavismo-duplico-el-numero-empleados-publicos/
    (2017315)
Iran, 2016, Iran (Islamic Republic of)'s Constitution of 1972
    with amendments through 1989: Constitute, (constitute
    project.org), 48 p.
Jeffco Public Schools, 2014, 2014/2015 Budget: Jefferson
    County, Colorado, 405 p. See:
    http://www.jeffcopublicschools.org/finance/documents/2
    014_15/2014-2015%20Adopted%20Budget_FINAL.pdf
    (2017228)
Jenks, C.L., 2004, The well-being of social systems: Systems
    Research and Behavioral Science, v. 21, n. 3, p. 209-217
Juffer, Femmie, van IJzendoorn, M.H., and Bakermans-
    Kranenburg, M.J.,2017, Structural neglect in orphanages:
    Physical growth, cognition, and daily life of young
    institutionalized children in India, in Rus A., Parris R., and
    Stativa E., eds., Child maltreatment in residential care:
    Springer, p. 301-321 See:
    https://link.springer.com/chapter/10.1007/978-3-319-
    57990-0_14
Khwaja, A.I., and Mian, Atif, 2005, Do lenders favor politically
    connected firms? Rent provision in an emerging financial
    market: The Quarterly Journal of Economics, v. 120, n. 4,
    p. 1371-1411
Klitgaard, Robert, and Light, P.C., eds., 2005, High-
    performance government: Structure, leadership,
    Incentives: Rand Corporation, 497 p.
Knott, J.H. and Miller, G.J., 1987, Reforming bureaucracy: The
    politics of institutional choice: Englewood Cliffs, NJ,
    Prentice Hall,

Korea, 2016, Korea (Democratic People's Republic)'s
    Constitution of 1972 with amendments through 1998:
    Constitute (constituteproject.org), 33 p.
Krafft, P.M., Zheng, Julia, et al., 2016, Human collective
    intelligence as distributed Bayesian inference: arXiv: 1608,
    01987v1, 6 Aug 2016, 25 p.
Landemore, Hélène, 2014a, Democracy as heuristic: The
    ecological rationality of political equality: Yale University,
    27 p.
Landemore, Hélène, 2014b, Yes, we can (Make It Up on
    Volume): Answers to critics: Yale University, 77 p.
Layard, Richard, 2016, Promoting happiness ethics: The
    greatest happiness principle, in John Helliwell, Richard
    Layard, and Jeffrey Sachs, eds., World happiness report
    2016, update, volume I: Sustainable Development Solution
    Network ,p. 50-55
Lupia, Arthur, 2016, Questioning our competence: Improving
    the practical relevance of political knowledge measures:
    University of Michigan, 67 p.
Meyer-Resende, Michael, 2011, International consensus:
    Essential elements of Democracy: Democracy Reporting
    International, 16 p. See:
    http://www.concernedhistorians.org/content_files/file/T
    O/333.pdf
Mitulya, Athuman, 2016, Tanzania: JPM enjoys 96pc approval
    rating—survey: All Africa, September 16th, 2016 See:
    http://allafrica.com/stories/201609160870.html
Moniruzzaman, M., 2018, Media and politics in Muslim world:
    Unfriendly relationship between press freedom and
    illiberal government: The Social Sciences, Medwell
    Journals, v. 3, n. 1, p. 70-79
Moore, J.M., (tr.), 1983, The constitution of the Athenians
    (ascribed to Xenophon) in Aristotle and Xenophon, On
    democracy and oligarchy: Berkeley, University of
    California Press, Translations with Introductions and
    Commentaries by J.M. Moore, p. 19-64
Nhat Hanh, Thich, 1999, The heart of the Buddha's teachings:
    New York, Broadway Books, 292 p.
NCEO, 2013, Open-Book management: The National Center
    for Employee Ownership. See:
    http://www.nceo.org/articles/open-book-management
    (2017220)

Needler, M.C., 1975, Military motivations in the seizure of power: Latin American Research Review, v. 10, n. 3, p. 63-79

Needler, M.C., 1978, The logic of conspiracy: The Latin American military coup as a problem in social sciences: University of New Mexico, Studies in Comparative International Development, v. 13, n. 2, p. 28-40

Niculae, Vlad, and Danescu-Nicolescu-Mizil, Cristian, 2016, Conversational markers of constructive discussions: Cornell University, arXive, 11 p.

OECD, 2013b, Key OECD anti-corruption documents. See: http://www.oecd.org/corruption/keyoecdanti-corruptiondocuments.htm (201398)

OGP (Open Government Partnership), 2011, Open government declaration: Open Government Partnership, September 2011 See: http://www.opengovpartnership.org/about/open-government-declaration (2017228)

Olken, B.A., and Pande, Rohini, 2012, Corruption in developing countries: MIT Economics Department, Annual Review of Economics 4, p. 479-505. See: http://economics.mit.edu/files/7589 (201293)

Pasquali, Jean, 2014a, Government and the society it serves: The difference between waiting for political decisions and making them: Arvada, Colorado, Mentation Publications, 284 p.

Pasquali, Jean, 2014b, El ciudadano toma su lugar: El gobierno mejora y la sociedad florece: Arvada, Colorado, Mentation Publications, 311 p.

Pasquali, Jean, 2017, De un día para otro: El Republicano Liberal, 2 p. See: http://elrepublicanoliberalii.blogspot.com/2017/03/jean-pasquali-de-un-dia-para-otro.html (2017313)

Peduzzi, Pascal, 2014, Sand, rarer than one thinks: UNEP, GEAS, 14 p. See: https://na.unep.net/geas/archive/pdfs/GEAS_Mar2014_Sand_Mining.pdf

Piketty, Thomas, 2014, Capital in the twenty-first century: Cambridge, The Belknap Press of Harvard University Press, 685 p.

Pomerol, Jean-Charles, and Adam, Frederic, 2004, Practical decision making—From the legacy of Herbert Simon to decision support systems: International Conference 2004, Decision support in an uncertain and complex world, 48 p.

Porter, M.E., Rivkin, J.W., et al., 2016, Problems unsolved: The state of U.S. competitiveness 2016: Harvard Business School, 70 p.

Priestland, David, 2013, Merchant, soldier, sage: A new history of the world in three castes: New York, The Penguin Press, p. 352

Qian, Zaijian, y Huo, Shitao, 2017, Politics of participation—Search for deliberation governance in China: Open Journal of Political Science, v. 7, p. 257-266

Repetti, R.L., Taylor, S.E., et al., 2002, Risky families: Family social environments and the mental and physical health of offspring: Psychological Bulletin, v. 128, n. 2, p. 330-366

Richter, L.M., Daelmans, Bernardette, et al., 2017, Investing in the foundation of sustainable development: pathways to scale up for early childhood development: The Lancet, v. 389, January 7, 2017, p. 103-118

Rosen, David, 2013, The 6 political personality types, 4 p. See: https://www.campaignsandelections.com/campaign-insider/the-6-political-personality-types (2016614)

Rouquié, Alain, 1987, The military and the state in Latin America: Berkeley, University of California Press, 469 p.

Roy, Jeffrey, 2016, Data, dialogue, and innovation: Opportunities and challenges for "Open Government" in Canada: Journal of Innovation Management, JIM 4, n. 1, p. 22-38

Seligman, M.E.P., 2004, Can happiness be taught? Daedalus, v. 133, n. 2, p. 26-33

Serrano, Martin, Boniface, Michael, et al., 2017, Next generation Internet research and experimentation: HAL Id: hal-01571407, 44p See: http://hal.upmc.fr/hal-01571417

Somin, Ilya, 2013a, Democracy and political ignorance: Why smaller government is smarter: Stanford University Press, 20 p.

Somin, Ilya, 2013b, Democracy and political ignorance: Cato Institute, October 11, 2013, 9p. See: http://www.cato-unbound.org/2013/10/11/ilya-somin/democracy-political-ignorance

Stolley, K.S., 2005, The basics of sociology: Westport, Connecticut, Greenwood Publishing Group, 302 p.

Tang, Wenfang, Lewis-Becky, M.S., and Martini, N.F., 2013, Government for people in China? The Diplomat, June 17th, 2013, 4 p. See: http://thediplomat.com/2013/06/government-for-the-people-in-china/

Tekinerdogan, Bedir, 2017, Engineering connected intelligence: A socio-technical perspective: Wageningen University, Inaugural Lecture, 44 p.

Transparency International, 2013, Corruption perception index 2012. See: http://www.transparency.org/cpi2012/results 2013812

Transparency International, 2016, Corruption perceptions index 2016. See: https://www.transparency.org/news/feature/corruption_ perceptions_index_2016 (2017626)

Transparency International, 2017, Global corruption barometer: Citizens's voices from around the world See: https://www.transparency.org/news/feature/global_corru ption_barometer_citizens_voices_from_around_the_wor ld?utm_medium=email&utm_campaign=Global%20News letter%2017%20November%202017&utm_content=Global %20Newsletter%2017%20November%202017+CID_84d3 561da476c62124d9591a20bb008f&utm_source=Email%2 0marketing%20software&utm_term=Global%20Corruptio n%20Barometer%20GCB (20171128)

UN, 2007, Guidance note of the Secretary-General on democracy, 9 p. See: http://www.un.org/democracyfund/sites/www.un.org.de mocracyfund/files/file_attach/UNSG%20Guidance%20No te%20on%20Democracy-EN.pdf (2017622)

UNDP, 2011, Human development index and its components. See: http://hdr.undp.org/en/statistics/hdi/

United Nations, 2006, Demographic yearbook. Divorces and crude divorce rates by urban/rural residence: 2002-2006. See: http://unstats.un.org/unsd/demographic/products/dyb/d yb2006/Table25.pdf (2013320)

United Nations, 2010, Life expectancy at birth: UNDP, United Nations Statistical Division, World Population Prospects: See: http://data.un.org/Data.aspx?d=GenderStat&f=inID%3A3 7 (2013510)

UNODC, 2012, 2011 Global study on homicide: United Nations
Office on Drugs and Crime, 128 p. See:
http://www.unodc.org/documents/data-and-
analysis/statistics/Homicide/Globa_study_on_homicide_
2011_web.pdf (201358)

UNODC, 2013, UNODC's action against corruption and
economic crime. See:
http://www.unodc.org/unodc/corruption/index.html
(201398)

UNODC, 2013a, Global study on homicide. Executive
summary, 11 p. See:
https://www.unodc.org/documents/gsh/pdfs/GLOBAL_
HOMICIDE_Report_ExSum.pdf (2017625)

UNohchr, 1976, International covenant on civil and political
rights. See:
http://www.ohchr.org/Documents/ProfessionalInterest/c
cpr.pdf (2017622)

UNU-IHDP and UNEP, 2012, Inclusive wealth report 2012.
Measuring progress towards sustainability: Cambridge,
Cambridge University Press, 368 p. See:
http://www.unep.org/pdf/IWR_2012.pdf (2013321)

Warnke, Philine, 2016, CIMULACT—Citizen and multi-actor
consultation on Horizon2020: Fraunhofer Institute for
Systems and Innovation Research ISI, 3 p. See:
http://www.isi.fraunhofer.de/isi-en/v/projekte/highlight-
projects/cimulact.php (2017228)

Weatherburn, Don, 2001, What causes crime?: NSW Bureau of
Crime, Statistics and Research, Crime and Justice Bulletin,
n. 54, 12 p. See:
http://www.lawlink.nsw.gov.au/lawlink/bocsar/ll_bocsar.
nsf/vwFiles/cjb54.pdf/$file/cjb54.pdf (201333)

Weiner, Eric, 2016, The geography of genius: New York, Simon
& Shuster, 353 p.

WHO (World Health Organization), 2004, Adolescent
pregnancy: WHO, 86 p.

WHO (World Health Organization), 2013, Global health
observatory: Life expectancy by country. See:
http://apps.who.int/gho/data/view.main.710 (2013321)

Williams, Rosie, 2016, Australia, where the bloody hell are
you??: On line Opinion, 4 p. See:
http://www.onlineopinion.com.au/view.asp?article=1808
3&page=0 (2016313)

Woolly, A.W., Chabris, C.F., Pentland, Alex, Hashmi, Nada, and Malone, T.W. 2010, Evidence for a collective intelligence factor in the performance of human groups: Science, v. 330, n. 6004, p. 686-688

World Bank, 2012, Costs & consequences of corruption See: http://web.worldbank.org/WBSITE/EXTERNAL/TOPICS/EXTPUBLICSECTORANDGOVERNANCE/EXTANTICORRUPTION/0,,contentMDK:20221941~menuPK:1165474~pagePK:148956~piPK:216618~theSitePK:384455,00.html (201359)

World Bank, 2013, What is our approach to anti-corruption? See: http://web.worldbank.org/WBSITE/EXTERNAL/WBI/EXTWBIGOVANTCOR/0,,contentMDK:20678938~pagePK:64168445~piPK:64168309~theSitePK:1740530,00.htm (2013812)

Yoinfluyo, 2017, Código de ética: Fundación Yo Influyo A.C. See: http://yoinfluyo.com/codigo-de-etica (201728)

Note 1

Note 2